CONTENTS

ANGIE
The Rolling Stones

Video Lesson – 12 minutes, 39 seconds

Standard Tuning: (low to high) E–A–D–G–B–E
Key of A minor

Guitar Tone:

- steel-string acoustic guitar

Chords:
Intro/Verse:

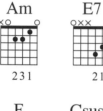

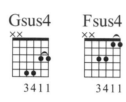

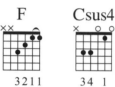

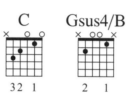

Chorus:

Techniques:

- Strum Variations: after you get the chords under your fingers, practice varying the strumming and picking on this tune. Change up the way you play the rhythms and arpeggios throughout so they are different than the notation. The Rolling Stones never play this chord structure the same way twice, and neither should you. There are endless variations possible and it's a great exercise in creativity and improvisation to generate as many as you can.

- Double Stops: fret the double stops by barring one finger across each fret. This will make the lick easier to grab as you move from chord strumming to fills and back.

- Harmonic: the very first note of the tune is a harmonic on the 12th fret of the A string. Lightly touch the string directly above the fret wire, without pushing down to the fretboard. Pluck the string and lift your finger off, allowing the harmonic to ring.

Angie

Words and Music by Mick Jagger and Keith Richards

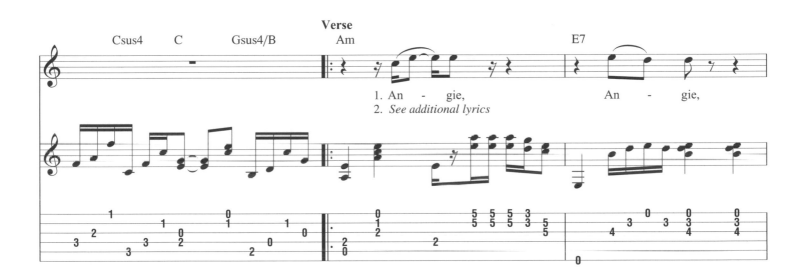

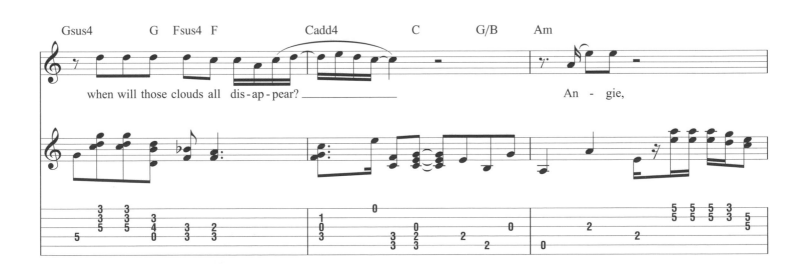

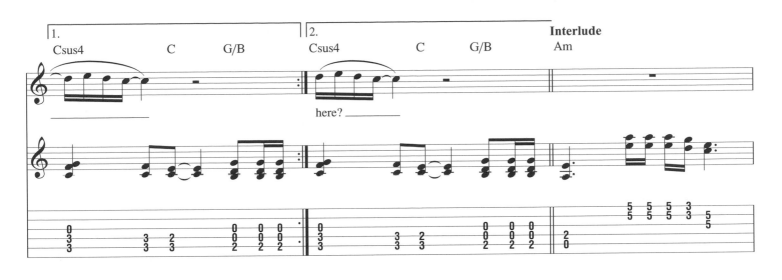

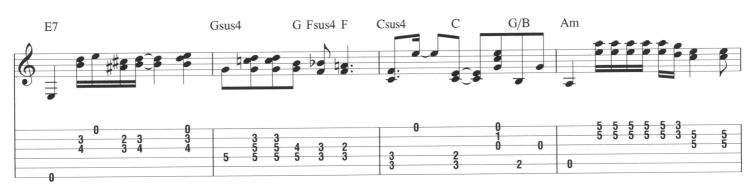

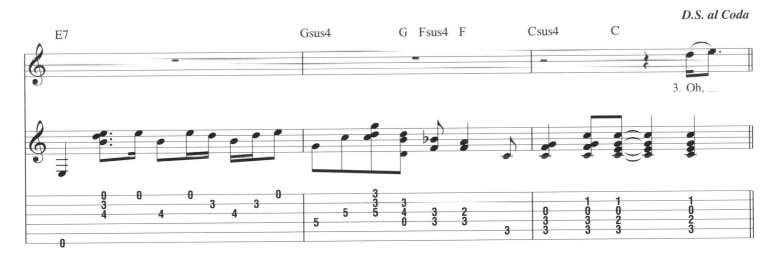

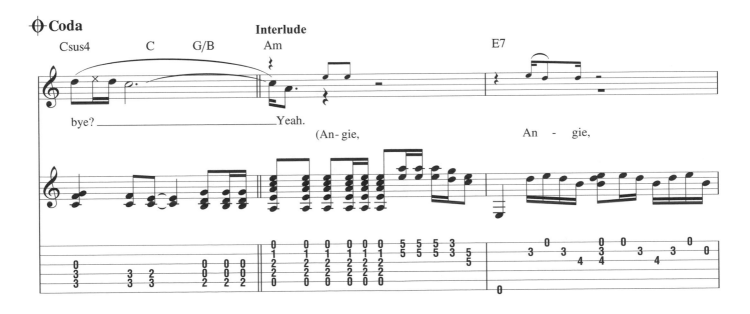

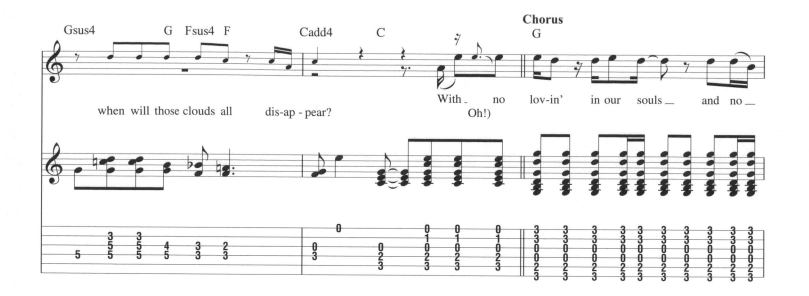

when will those clouds all dis-ap-pear?

Chorus

(Oh!) With no lov-in' in our souls and no

mon-ey in our coats, uh, you can't say we're sat-is-fied.

Bridge

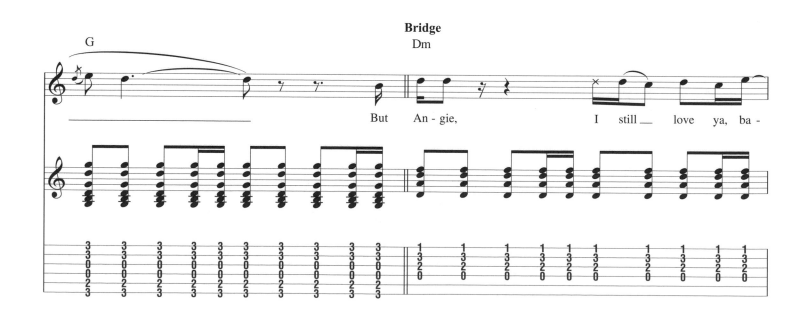

But An-gie, I still love ya, ba-

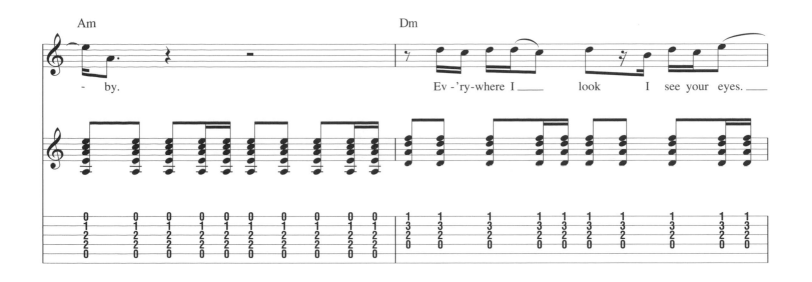

Verse

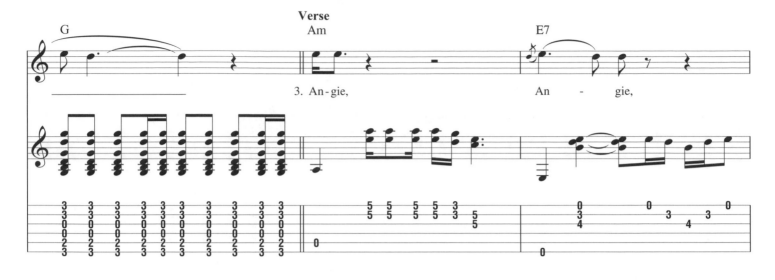

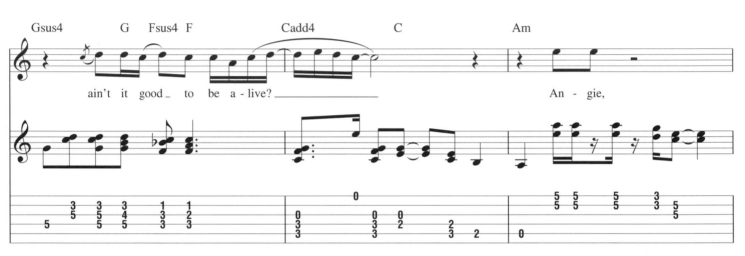

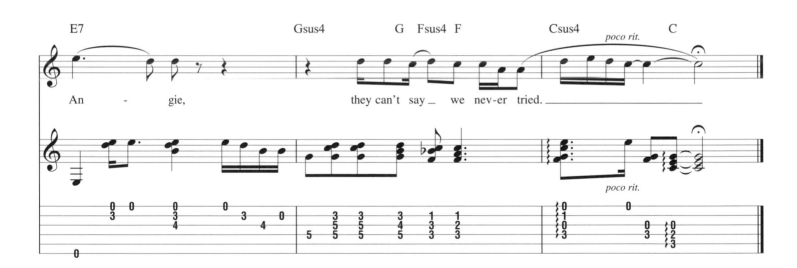

Additional Lyrics

2. A-Angie, you're beautiful, yes,
But ain't it time we said goodbye?
A-Angie, I still love ya.
Remember all those nights we cried?

Chorus 2. All the dreams we held so close
Seemed to all go up in smoke.
Uh, let me whisper in your ear.
Whispered: Angie, Angie,
Where will it lead us from here?

Chorus 3. Oh, Angie, don't you weep,
All your kisses still taste sweet.
I hate that sadness in your eyes.
But Angie, Angie,
A-ain't it time we said goodbye?

DAUGHTERS
John Mayer

Video Lesson – 21 minutes, 20 seconds

Standard Tuning: (low to high) E–A–D–G–B–E
Key of D

Guitar Tone:

- acoustic guitar or clean tone electric
- light reverb

Chords:

Verse 1:

Bm11   Em7   A7sus$^2_4$ D

Chorus:

E7

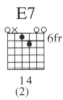

Verse 2:

Bm   Em7   A7sus4   F#m7

   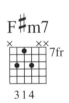

Bridge:

Am/D   Gm   D   A13

   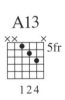

A7   Bm11   Em7   Dadd9/F#

Gm9   A7   Dadd4/A   A7(no3rd)   A13(no3rd)

    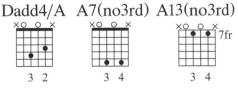

Scales/Arpeggios:

Intro/Interlude:

D Major Scale

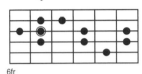

6fr

Techniques:

- Strumming: for the Verse and Chorus, strum the eighth note with a downstroke, and the sixteenth notes with alternating down-up-down-up strokes.

- Vibrato: shake the note up and down, creating a little series of quick bends and releases. Be sure to keep your wrist loose!

- Thumb-Fretting: some of the chords in the song involve fretting the 6th string with your thumb. This allows for more use of the other fingers. If this technique isn't comfortable for you, feel free to fret the chords with the other fret-hand fingers.

- String Bending: bending on an acoustic can be tough! Make sure you use support fingers behind the fretted note.

- Open-String Chords: be sure to stand your fret-hand fingers up straight for the arpeggiated chords in the last two measures of the Bridge. Make sure those open strings are ringing clearly and not getting muted by a flattened finger.

Daughters

Words and Music by John Mayer

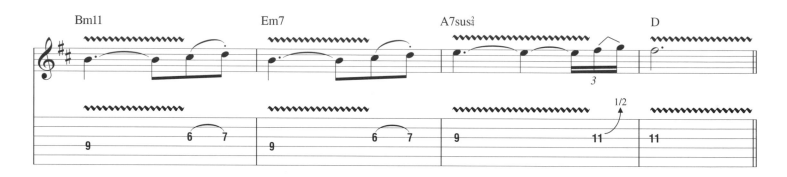

*Played as even sixteenth notes.

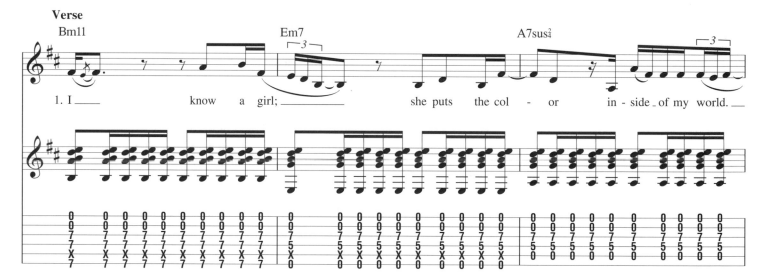

1. I ____ know a girl; ____ she puts the col - or in - side of my world. ____

____ But she's just like a maze ____ where all of the walls ____

Daugh-ters will love _ like you do. _____ Girls be-come _ lov-ers who

To Coda 1

To Coda 2

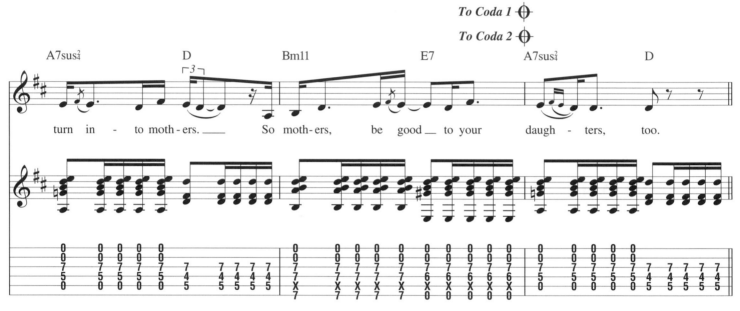

turn in - to moth-ers. _____ So moth-ers, be good _ to your daugh - ters, too.

Interlude

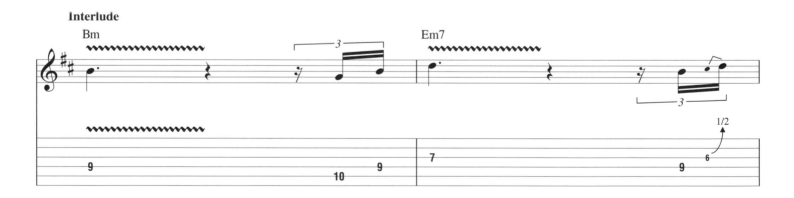

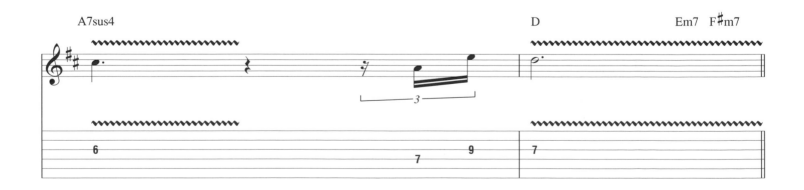

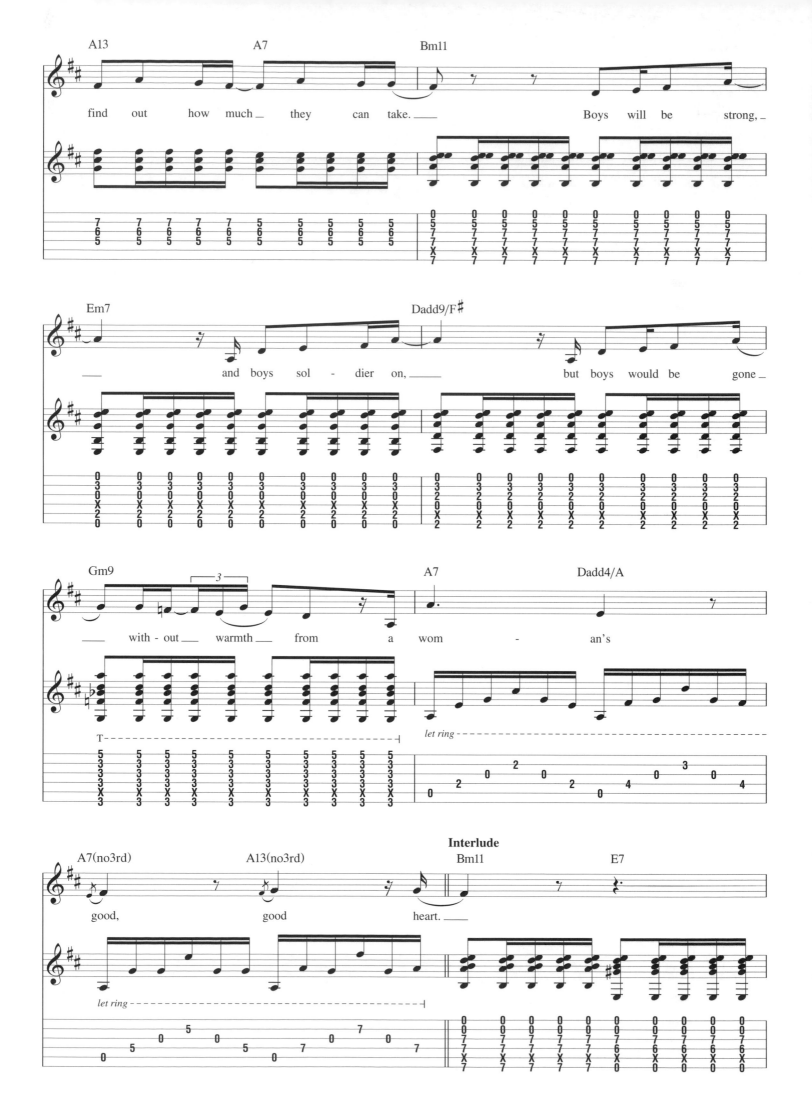

DRIVE
Incubus

Video Lesson – 9 minutes, 35 seconds

Standard Tuning: (low to high) E–A–D–G–B–E
Key of E minor

Guitar Tone:

- Guitar Tone 1:
  - ❭ acoustic guitar or clean tone electric
  - ❭ light reverb

- Guitar Tone 2 (Interlude):
  - ❭ electric guitar
  - ❭ light distortion
  - ❭ light reverb
  - ❭ Leslie effect
  - ❭ bridge pickup
  - ❭ EQ: bass – 5, mid – 6, treble – 7

Chords:

Intro:

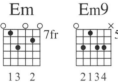 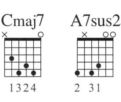

Em	Em9	Cmaj7	A7sus2
7fr	5fr		
13 2	2134	1324	2 31

Pre-Chorus:

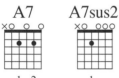

A7	A7sus2
1 2	1

Techniques:

- Muted Strums: keep your fret hand lightly in contact with the strings, being careful not to accidentally fret any notes by pressing down too hard. Strum the muted strings, producing a "click" type sound. You can also assist the damping by using your pick hand to palm mute the strings near the bridge.

- Open-String Chords: most of the chords in this song involve a mixture of fretted notes and open strings. Make sure to fret these with the tips of your fret-hand fingers, allowing the open strings to ring clearly.

- Grace-Note Hammer-Ons/Slides: for the single-note solo in the Interlude, the small-sized grace notes don't have any rhythmic value, so move on to the attached second note as quickly as possible (whether it's a hammer-on or slide). Grace notes are also indicated with smaller numbers in the tab.

- Pick Slide: at the end of the last Pre-Chorus, you'll encounter a pick slide. Rub the edge of your pick down the strings, producing a scratchy sound. This will create ridges in the pick, so use an area of it that you don't typically employ for picking the strings.

Drive

Words and Music by Brandon Boyd, Michael Einziger, Alex Katunich, Jose Pasillas II and Chris Kilmore

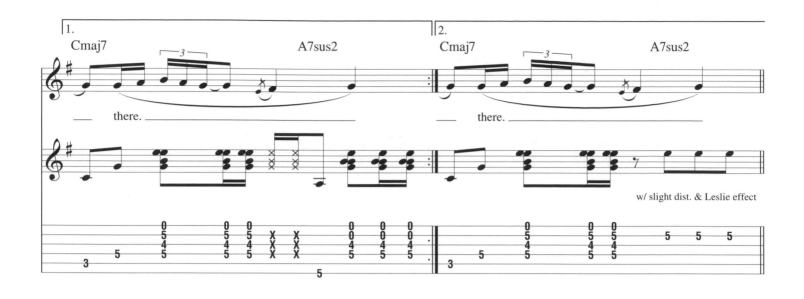

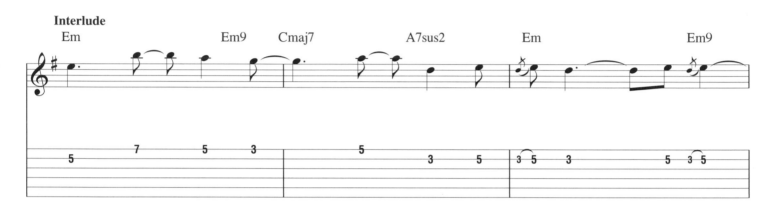

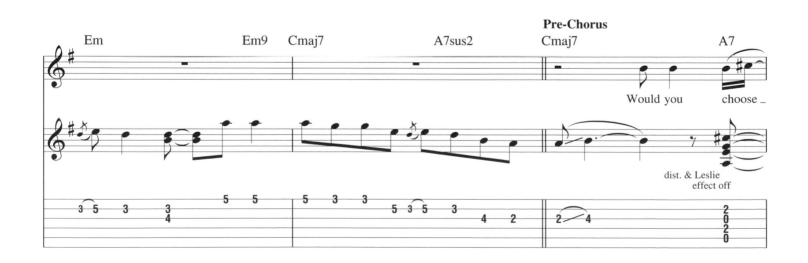

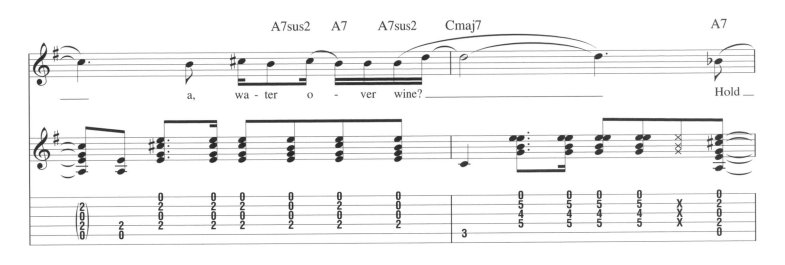

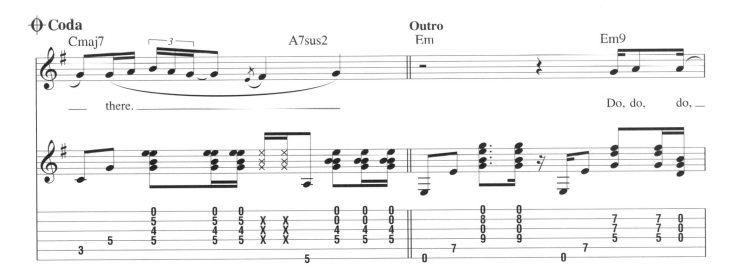

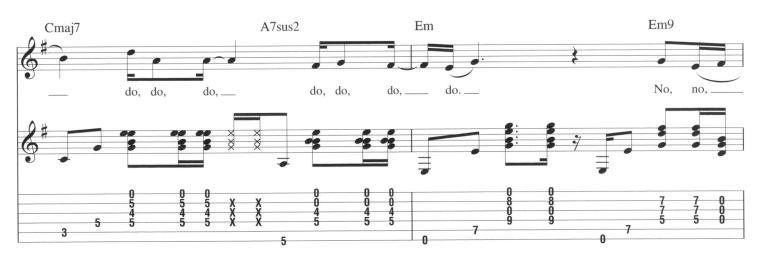

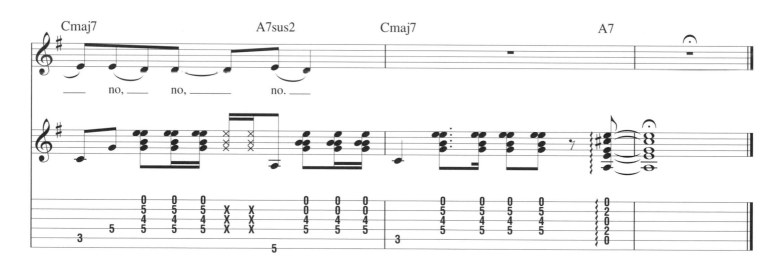

Additional Lyrics

2. So if I decide to waiver the
   Chance to be one of the hive,
   Will I choose water over wine
   And hold my own and drive?
   Oh, oh, oh.

Pre-Chorus It's driven me before,
   And it seems to be the way,
   That ev'ryone else gets around.
   But lately I'm beginning to find
   That when I drive myself my light is found.

IRIS
Goo Goo Dolls

Video Lesson – 20 minutes, 31 seconds

Tuning: (low to high) B–D–D–D–D–D
Key of D

Guitar Tone:

- acoustic guitar or clean tone electric

- light reverb

Chords:

Intro:

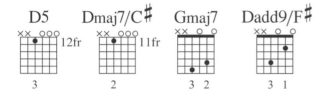

Verse:

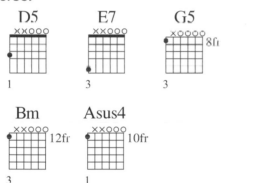

Interlude/Guitar Solo:

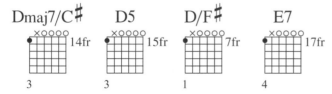

Techniques:

- Alternate Tuning: this song uses a very unique tuning. If you stick with your normal set of strings, be careful when fretting the strings that are tuned down. Use light pressure and make sure to not accidentally bend the now looser strings.

- Open-String Chords: all of the chords in this song involve a mixture of fretted notes and open strings. Make sure to fret these with the tips of your fret-hand fingers, allowing the open strings to ring clearly.

- Arpeggios: for the arpeggio section in the Verse, pick the first note with a downstroke and then catch the next three with an upstroke. Repeat this pattern for each new chord.

- Odd Time Signatures: the song moves from 8/8 to 12/8 and 6/8. Be sure to count or feel those meter changes.

- Muted Notes: when strumming the chords during the Guitar Solo, fret with a slightly flattened or angled finger, allowing the 5th string to be muted. Strum right through all six strings.

Iris

from the Motion Picture CITY OF ANGELS
Words and Music by John Rzeznik

Tuning:
(low to high) B♭-D♭-D-D♭-D♭-D

Intro

Moderately slow ♩. = 51

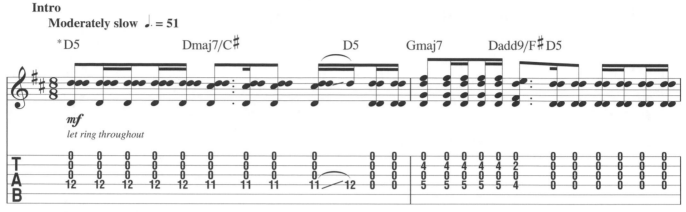

*Chord symbols reflect implied harmony.

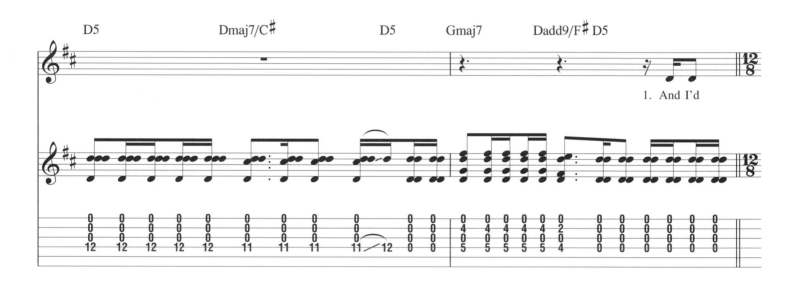

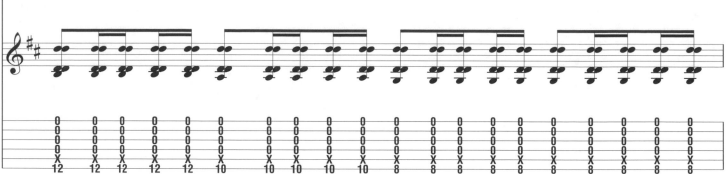

don't want the world ____ to see ____ me 'cause I don't _

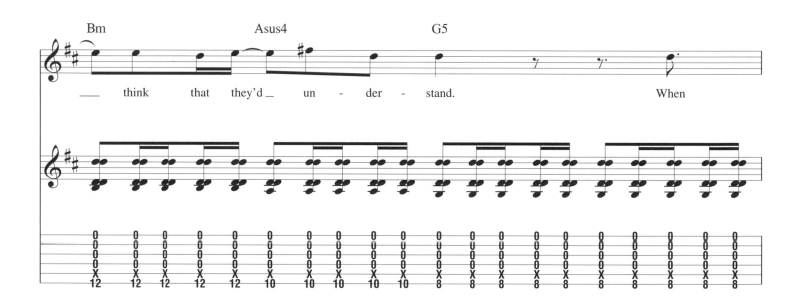

____ think that they'd _ un - der - stand. When

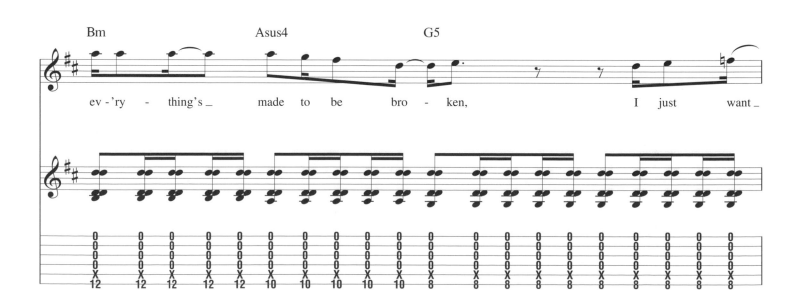

ev -'ry - thing's _ made to be bro - ken, I just want _

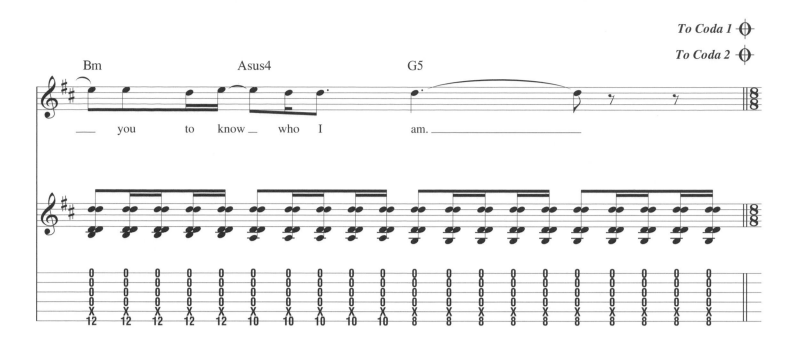

you to know who I am.

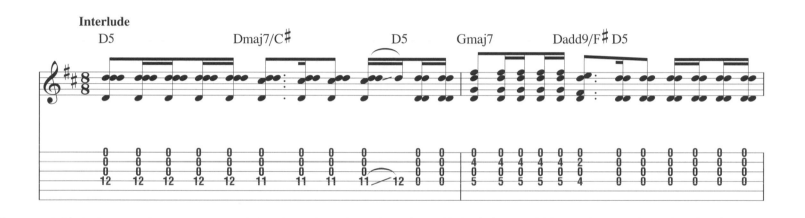

Interlude

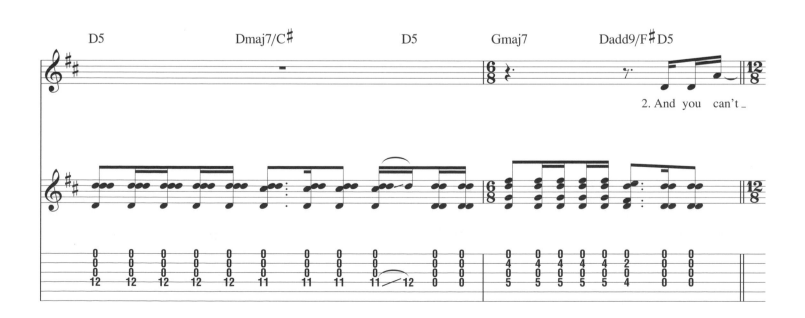

2. And you can't

Verse

_____ fight the tears _ that ain't com-in'   or the mo - ment of truth _ in your lies. _   When

D.S. al Coda 1

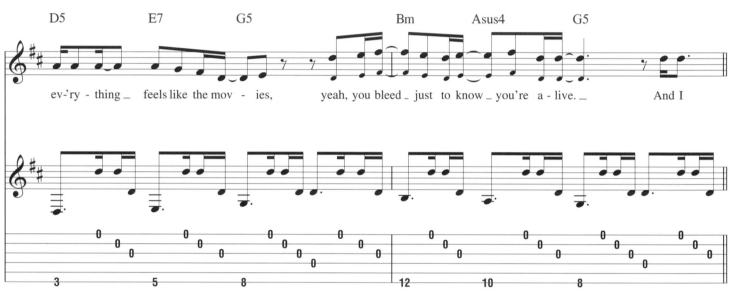

ev-'ry - thing _ feels like the mov - ies,   yeah, you bleed _ just to know _ you're a - live. _   And I

Coda 1

Interlude

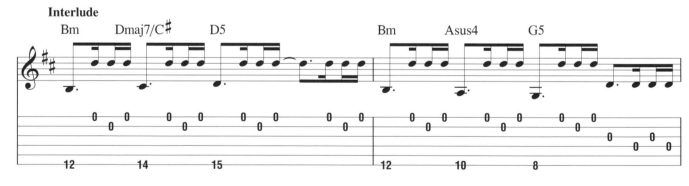

— 30 —

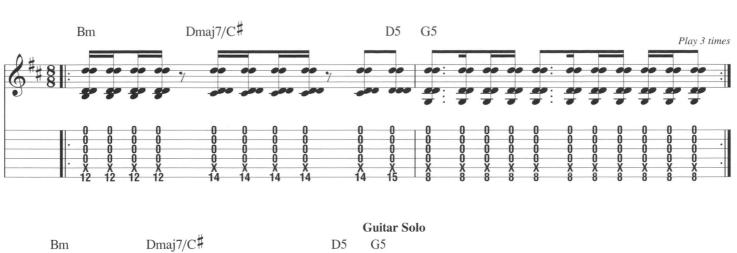

Guitar Solo

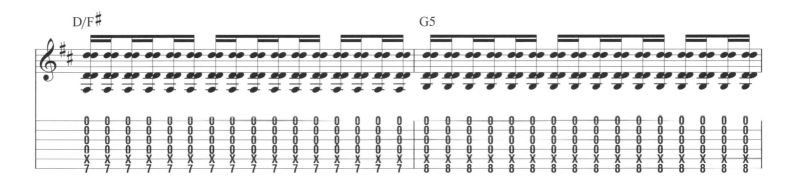

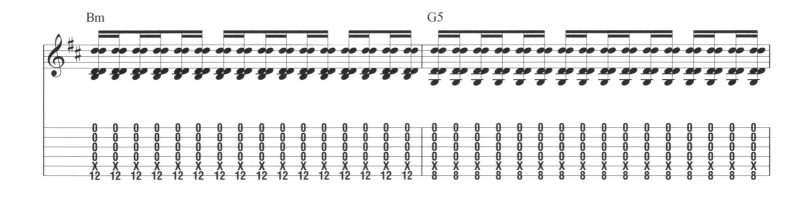

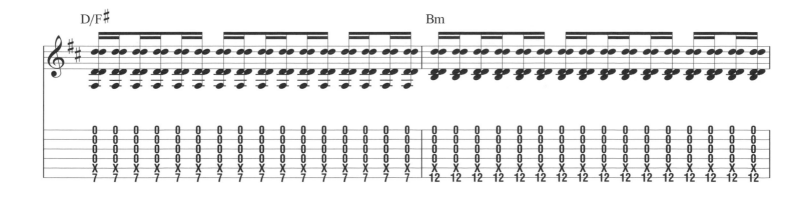

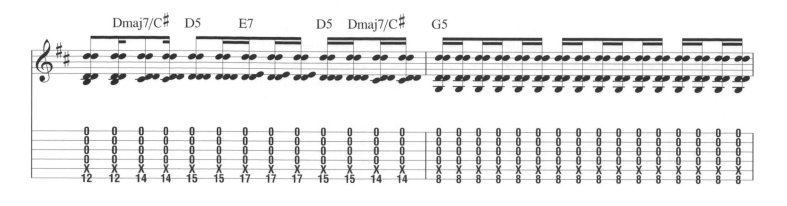
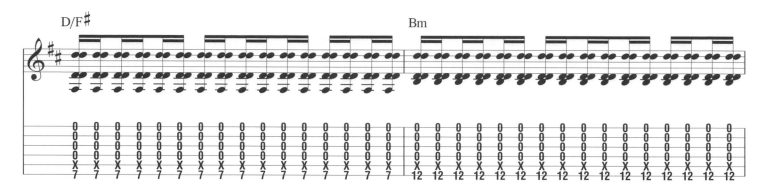
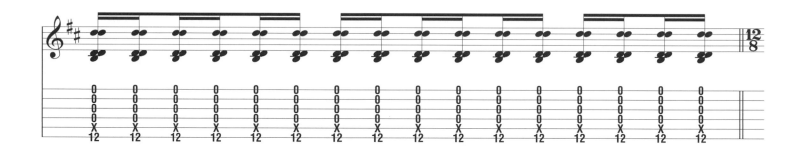
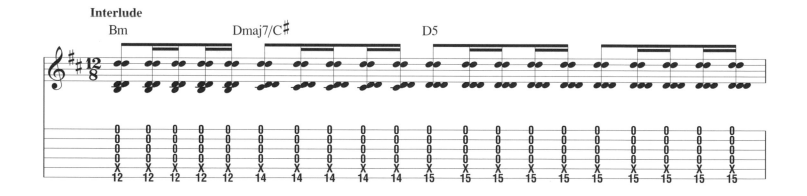
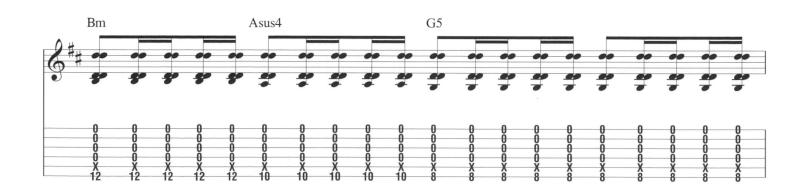

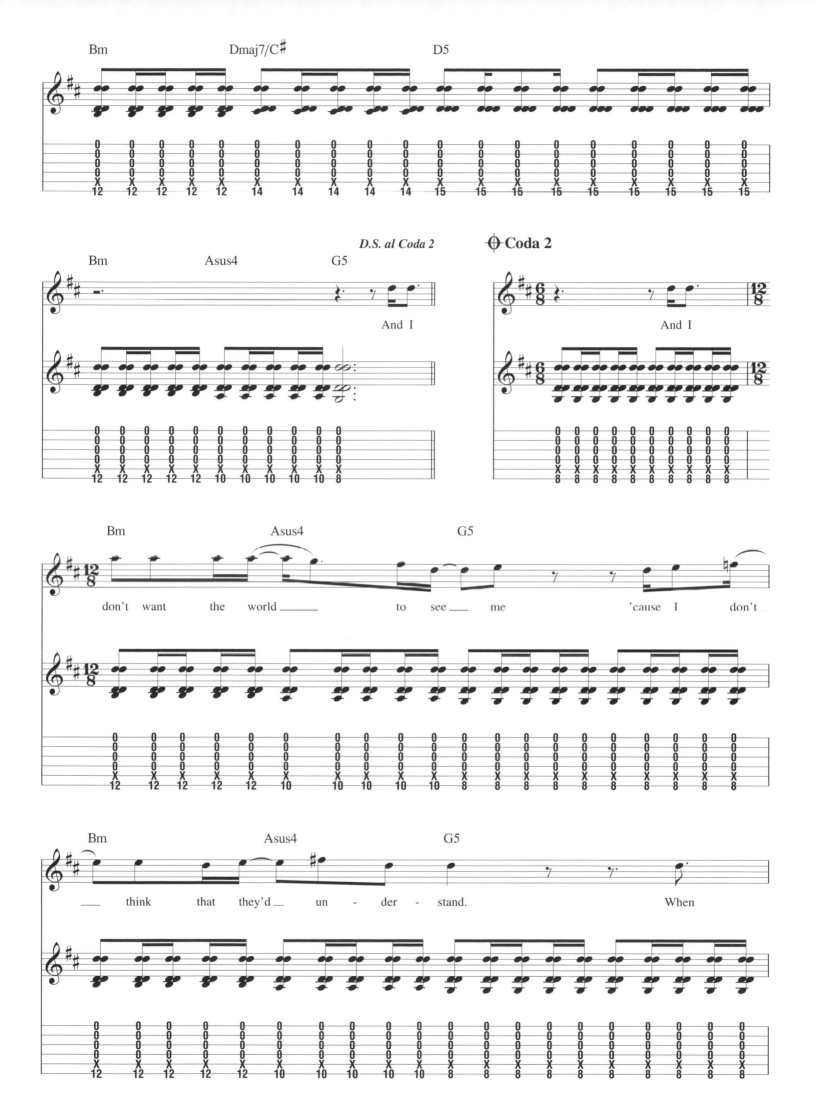

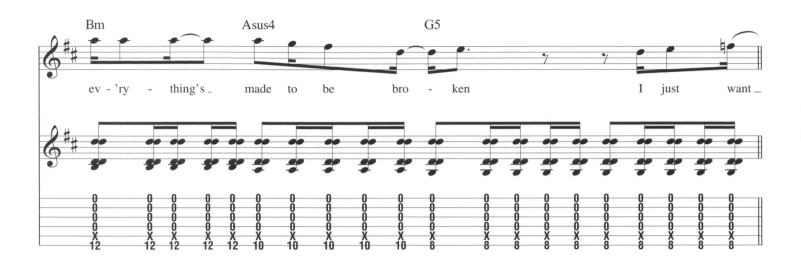

ev - 'ry - thing's _ made to be bro - ken   I just   want _

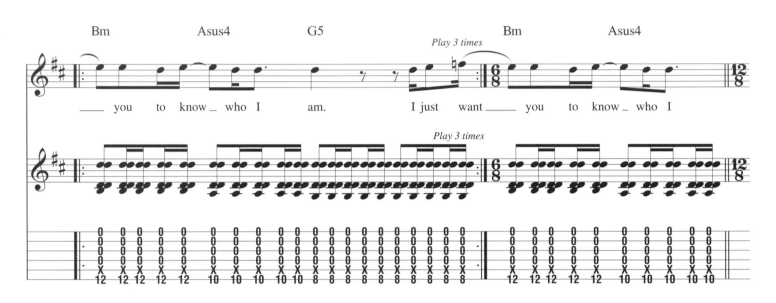

_____ you   to   know _ who   I   am.   I just   want _____ you   to   know _ who   I

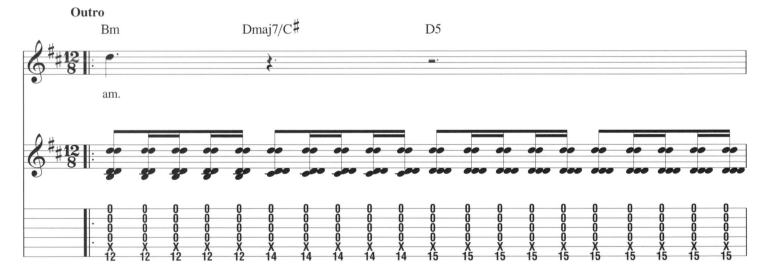

Outro

am.

Repeat and fade

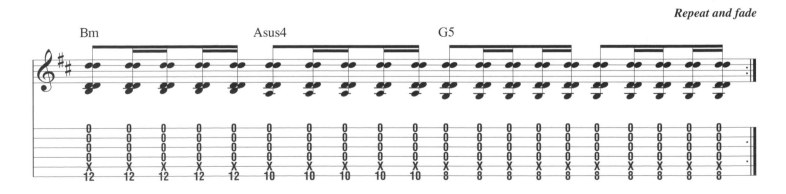

LAYLA (UNPLUGGED)
Eric Clapton

Video Lesson – 17 minutes, 32 seconds

Standard Tuning: (low to high) E–A–D–G–B–E
Key of D minor, C♯ minor

Guitar Tone:

- acoustic guitar or clean tone electric
- light reverb

Chords:

Intro:

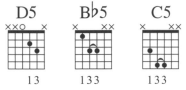

D5   B♭5   C5
13   133   133

Verse:

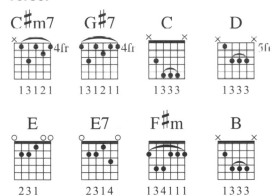

C♯m7   G♯7   C   D
13121 131211 1333 1333

E   E7   F♯m   B
231 2314 134111 1333

A
123

Techniques:

- Hammer-Ons/Pull-Offs: for hammer-ons, strike the first note and then come down forcefully with your fret-hand finger to sound the next note. For the pull-off, strike the first note while also fretting the second note below. Pull off in a slightly downward motion, allowing the second note to ring. Be careful not to sound the higher string with your pull-off finger.

- Vibrato: Clapton is a master of vibrato. Shake the note up and down, creating a little series of quick bends and releases. Vary the intensity and speed of the vibrato in accordance to the phrasing of the solo. Be sure to keep your wrist loose!

- Barre Chords: keep your 1st finger straight and flat and make sure all fretted notes ring clearly. You might find it helpful to roll your 1st finger a bit to the outside (towards the thumb) to help it remain flat.

- String Bending: bending on an acoustic can be tough! Make sure you use support fingers behind the fretted note.

Scales/Arpeggios:

Guitar Solos:

D Minor Pentatonic Scale

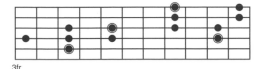

3fr

Layla

Words and Music by Eric Clapton and Jim Gordon

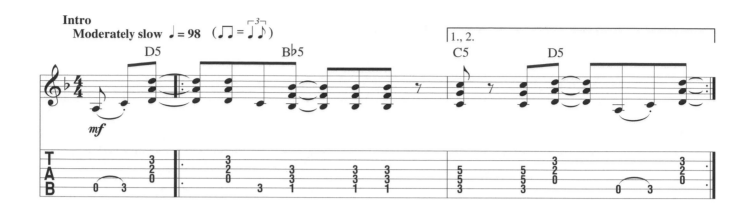

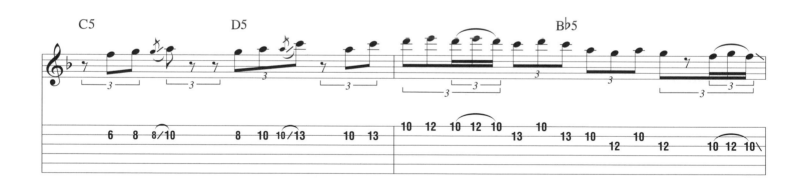

Verse

2. Tried to give you __ con-so-la-tion,
3. *See additional lyrics*

dar-lin' won't you ease my wor-ried mind? __

your old man had let you down. __ Like __ a __ fool, I

fell in love __ with you. You turned my whole world up-side down. Lay-la, __

beg - gin' dar - lin', please. Lay - la, _____

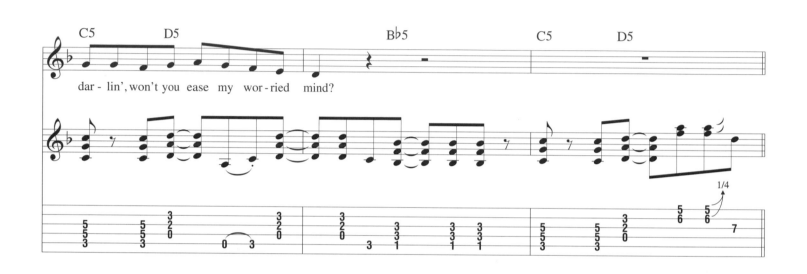

dar - lin', won't you ease my wor - ried mind?

Guitar Solo

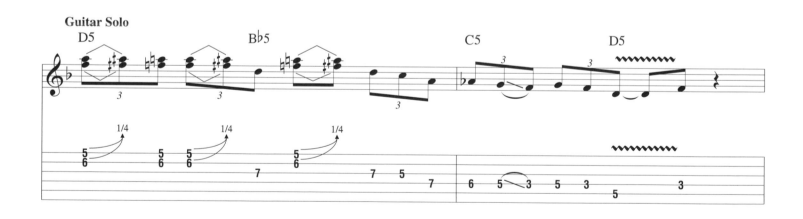

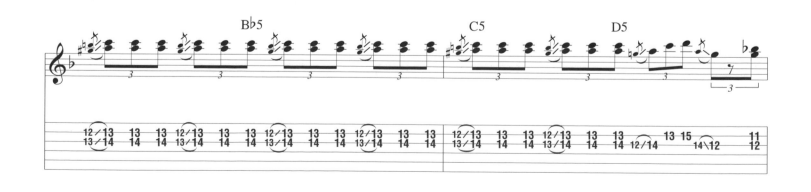

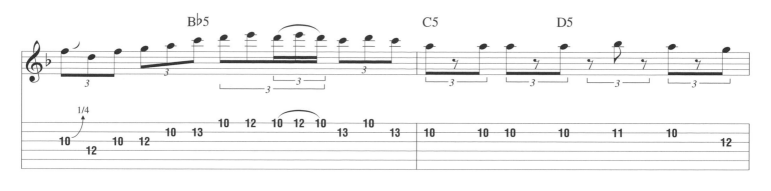

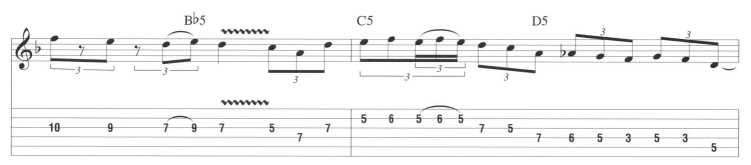

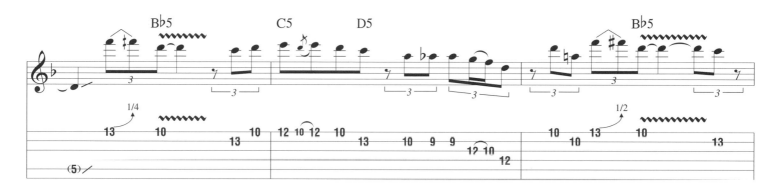

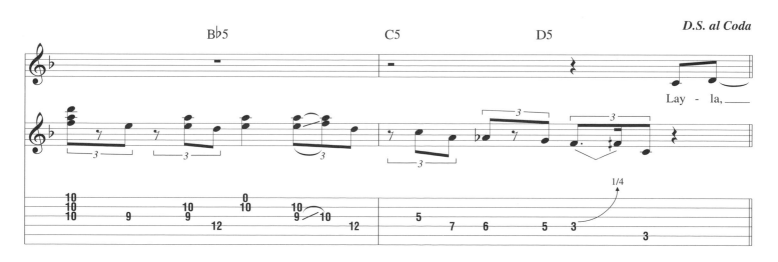

Additional Lyrics

3. Make the best of the situation,
   Before I fin'ly go insane.
   Please don't say we'll never find a way.
   Tell me all my love's in vain.

MR. JONES
Counting Crows

Video Lesson – 9 minutes, 5 seconds

Standard Tuning: (low to high) E–A–D–G–B–E
Key of A minor, C

Guitar Tone:

- acoustic guitar or clean tone electric

- light reverb

Chords:
Intro/Verse:

Am   F   Dm   G5
231   134211   231   2   34

Chorus:

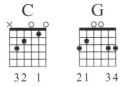

C   G
32 1   21   34

Bridge:

Fmaj7
T3421

Techniques:

- Open-Position Chords: make sure all the open strings ring clearly. If not, you might need to fret more on your fingertips so you aren't unintentionally muting any strings.

- Barre Chords: keep your 1st finger straight and flat and make sure all fretted notes ring clearly. You might find it helpful to roll your 1st finger a bit to the outside (towards the thumb) to help it remain flat.

- Thumb-Fretting: for the Fmaj7 chord in the Bridge, fret the low F on the 6th string with the side of your fret-hand thumb. You may have to adjust your normal fret-hand position to make this comfortable.

- Muted Strums: keep your fret hand lightly in contact with the strings, being careful not to accidentally fret any notes by pressing down too hard. Strum the muted strings, producing a "click" type sound. You can also assist the damping by using your pick hand to palm mute the strings near the bridge.

Mr. Jones

Words and Music by Adam Duritz, David Bryson, Charles Gillingham, Matthew Malley, Steve Bowman, Daniel Vickrey and Ben Mize

Chorus

Be - lieve ___ in me ___ Help me be - lieve in an - y - thing I ___

___ want to be some - one who be - lieves ___

1. Mis - ter Jones and ___ me tell each oth - er fair -
2., 3. See additional lyrics

y tales ___ Stare at the beau - ti - ful wom - en "She's look -

— 48 —

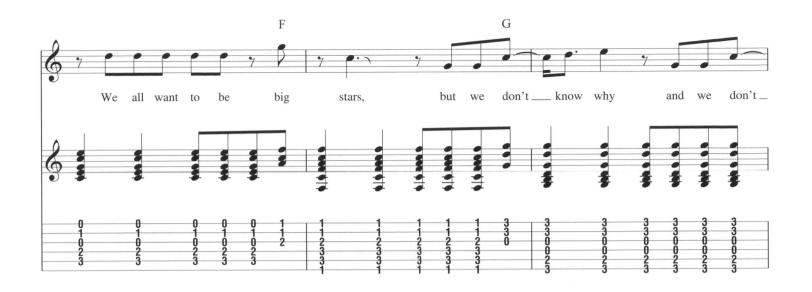

We all want to be big stars, but we don't __ know why __ and we don't __

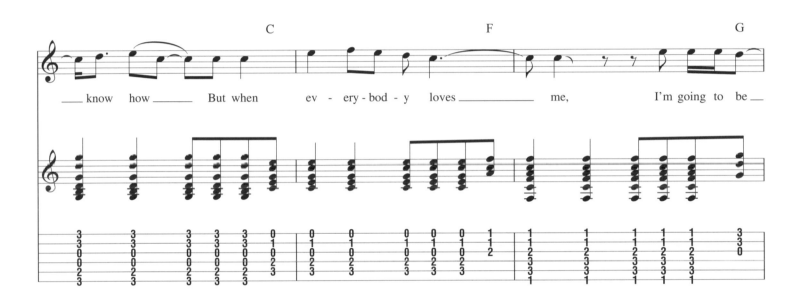

__ know how __ But when ev - ery - bod - y loves __ me, I'm going to be __

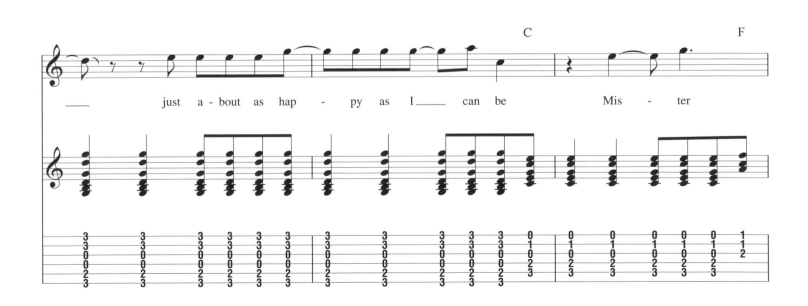

__ just a - bout as hap - py as I __ can be Mis - ter

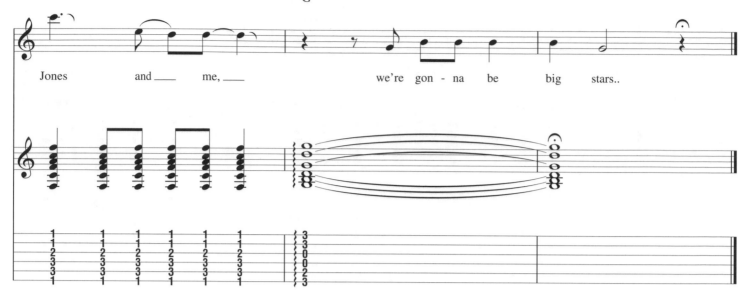

Jones and me, we're gon-na be big stars..

Additional Lyrics

3. I will paint my picture
   Paint myself in blue and red and black and gray
   All of the beautiful colors are very very meaningful
   Gray is my favorite color
   I felt so symbolic yesterday
   If I knew Picaso I would buy myself a gray guitar and play

Chorus 2. Mr. Jones and me look into the future
   Stare at the beautiful women
   "She's looking at you.
   Uh, I don't think so. She's looking at me."
   Standing in the spotlight
   I bought myself a gray guitar
   When everybody loves me, I will never be lonely

Chorus 3. Mr. Jones and me stumbling through the barrio
   Yeah we stare at the beautiful women
   "She's perfect for you, Man, there's got to be
   somebody for me."
   I wanna be Bob Dylan
   Mr. Jones wishes he was someone just a little more
   funky
   When everybody loves you, son, that's just about as
   funky as you can be

MORE THAN WORDS
Extreme

Video Lesson – 22 minutes, 30 seconds

Tune Down 1/2 Step: (low to high) E♭–A♭–D♭–G♭–B♭–E♭
Key of G

Guitar Tone:

- steel-string or nylon-string acoustic guitar
- medium reverb

Chords:

Intro:

G

G/B

Cadd9

Am7

C

D

Dsus4

Verse:

Em

D7

D/F♯

Dadd2/F♯

Chorus:

G7

Cm

Em7

Bm

Techniques:

- **Pick-Hand Slap:** throughout almost the entire song, the pick hand slaps the strings on beats 2 and 4. Instead of slapping with an open hand, come down in position ready to pluck the next chord.

- **Fingerstyle:** put your pick away for this one, it's played exclusively with the fingers! If this is a new technique for you, keep the fingers lightly arched and pluck the strings with the fingers moving towards the palm, in a piano (or block) style of picking.

- **Guitar Body Slap:** slap the body of the guitar with your pick hand, either behind the bridge or on the upper bout.

- **Thumb-Fretting:** for the D/F♯ and Dadd2/F♯, fret the F♯ on the 6th string with the side of your fret-hand thumb. You may have to adjust your normal fret-hand position to make this comfortable.

- **Two-Handed Tapping:** the free time ending features some two-handed tapping. Use either the index or middle finger of the pick hand to tap the notes at the indicated frets.

- **Neck Bend:** this is not a recommended technique! But if you want to try and emulate the sound on the original recording, gently grab your headstock with your fret hand while creating opposing pressure with your pick hand just above where the neck joins the body. Lightly push in opposite directions. The key term is *lightly*!

More Than Words

Words and Music by Nuno Bettencourt and Gary Cherone

Tune down 1/2 step:
(low to high) Eb-Ab-Db-Gb-Bb-Eb

Intro
Moderately slow ♩ = 96

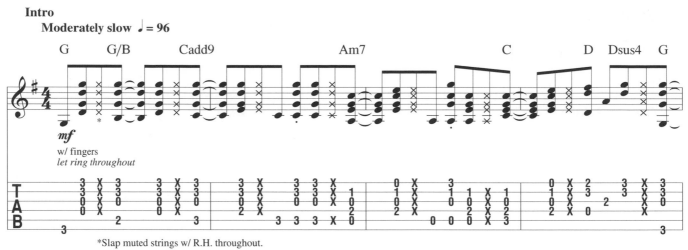

*Slap muted strings w/ R.H. throughout.

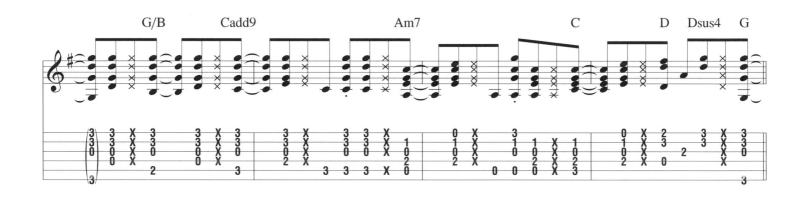

Verse

1. Say-ing "I ___ love ___ you" is not the words _ I want _

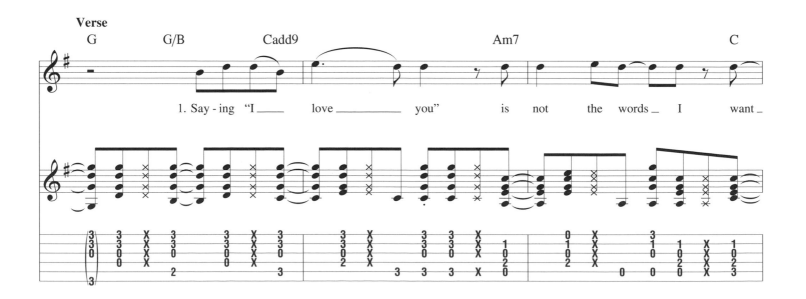

to — hear — from — you. It's not that I — want — you

not to say, — but if — you — on - ly — knew — how —

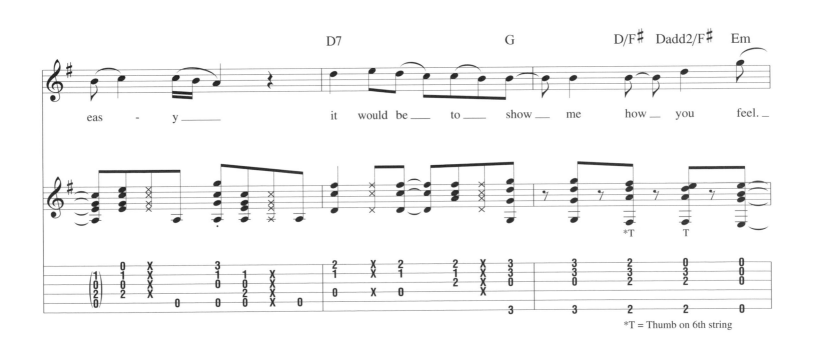

eas - y — it would be — to — show — me how — you feel. —

*T = Thumb on 6th string

Chorus

More than words _____ is all you have _ to __ do _

___ to make _ it ___ real. ___ Then you would - n't have _ to say _

___ that you love __ me, _ 'cause I'd _____ al - read - y _____

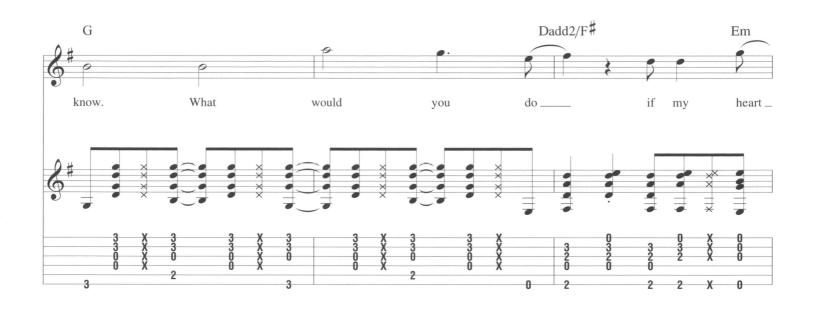

know. What would you do ___ if my heart ___

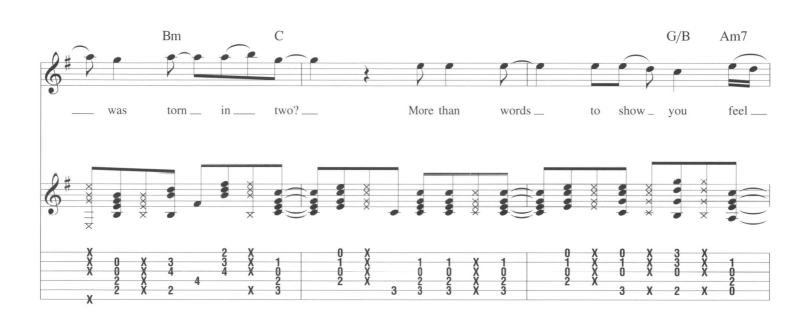

___ was torn ___ in ___ two? ___ More than words ___ to show ___ you feel ___

___ that your love ___ for me ___ is ___ real. ___ What

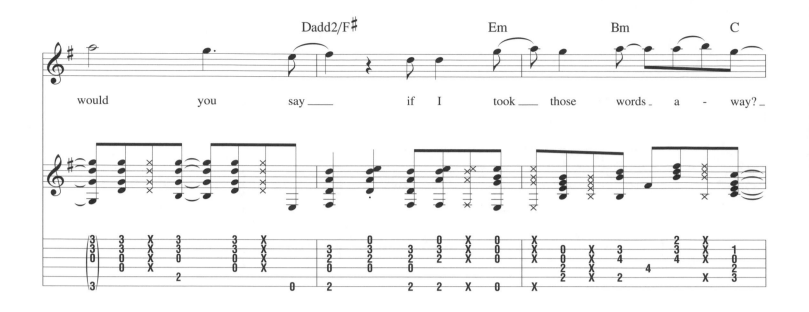

would you say ___ if I took ___ those words ___ a - way? ___

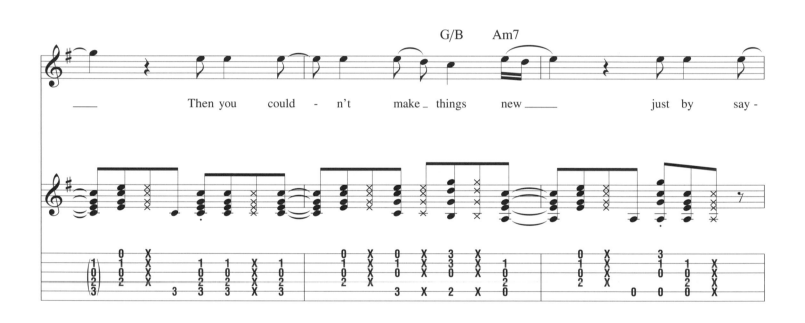

___ Then you could - n't make ___ things new ___ just by say-

Interlude

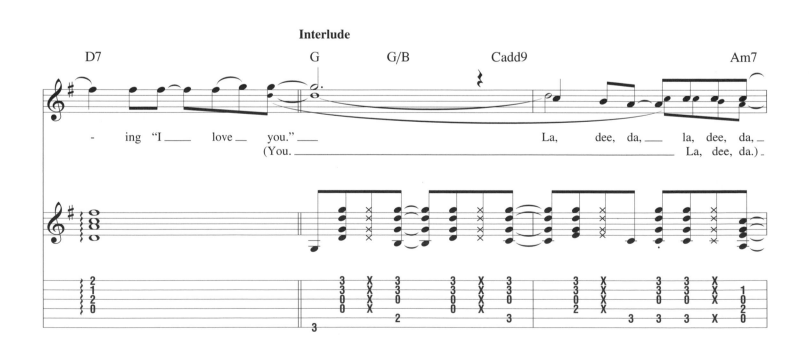

- ing "I ___ love ___ you." ___   La,   dee,   da, ___ la,   dee,   da, ___
(You. ___   La,   dee,   da.) ___

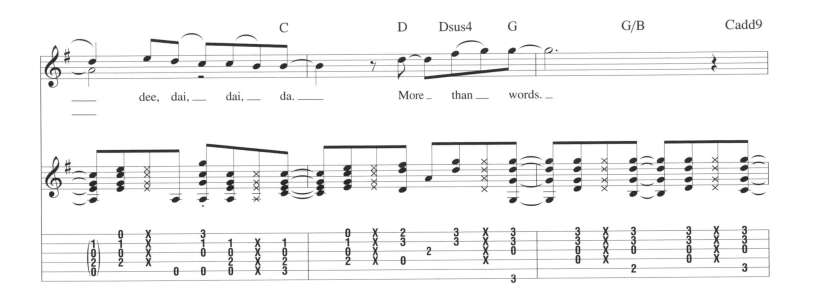

dee, dai, ___ dai, ___ da. ___ More ___ than ___ words. ___

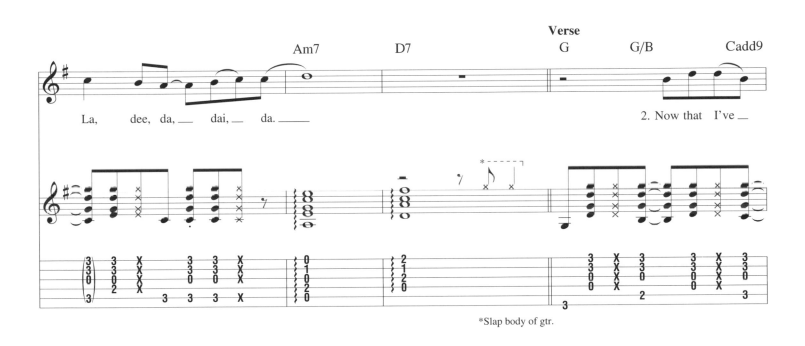

La, dee, da, ___ dai, ___ da. ___

2. Now that I've ___

*Slap body of gtr.

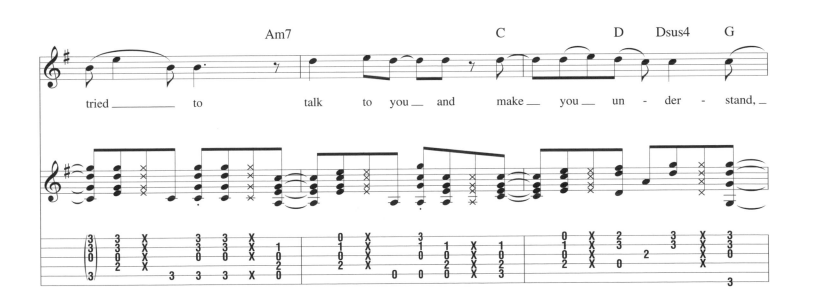

tried _____ to talk to you ___ and make ___ you ___ un - der - stand, ___

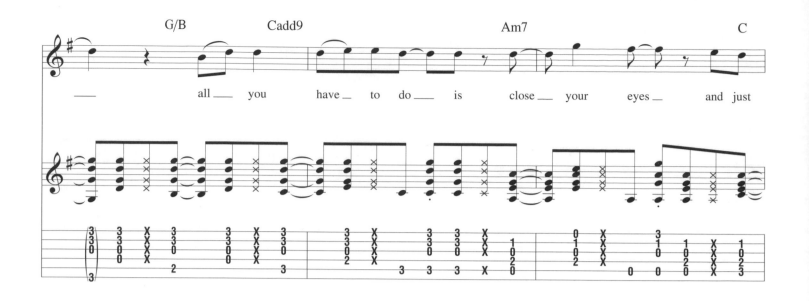

all ___ you have ___ to do ___ is close ___ your eyes ___ and just

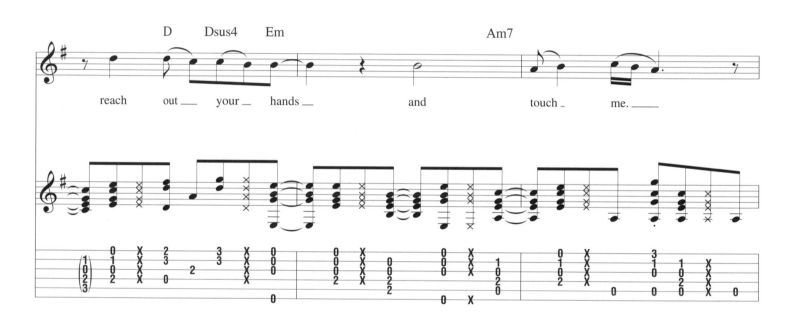

reach out ___ your ___ hands ___ and touch ___ me. ___

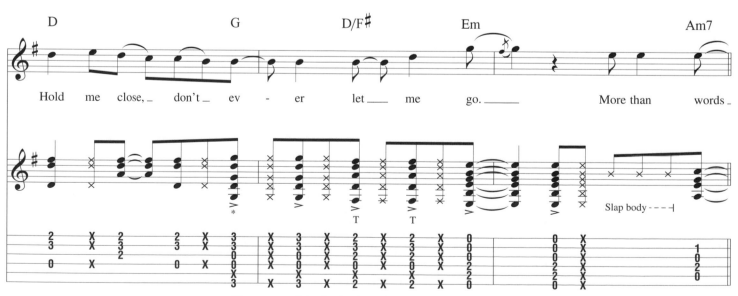

Hold me close, ___ don't ___ ev - er let ___ me go. ___ More than words ___

*Strum accented chords w/ nails (all downstrokes);
hit muted strings w/ R.H. as before.

Chorus

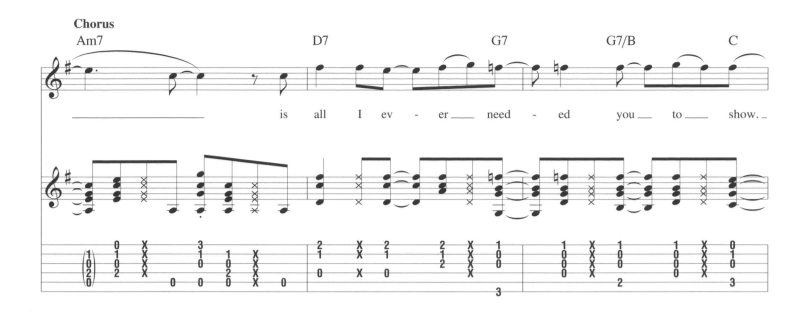

is all I ev - er ____ need - ed you ___ to ___ show. ___

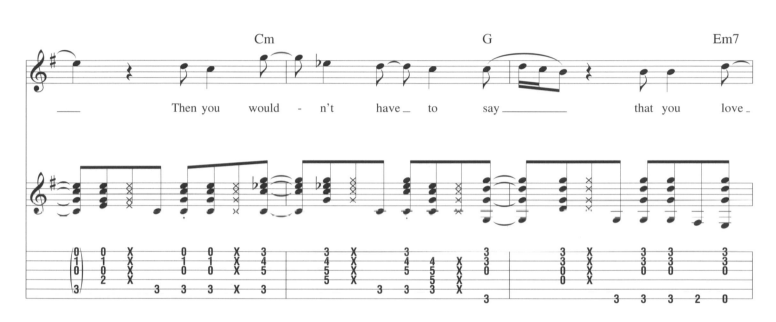

____ Then you would - n't have ___ to say _____ that you love ___

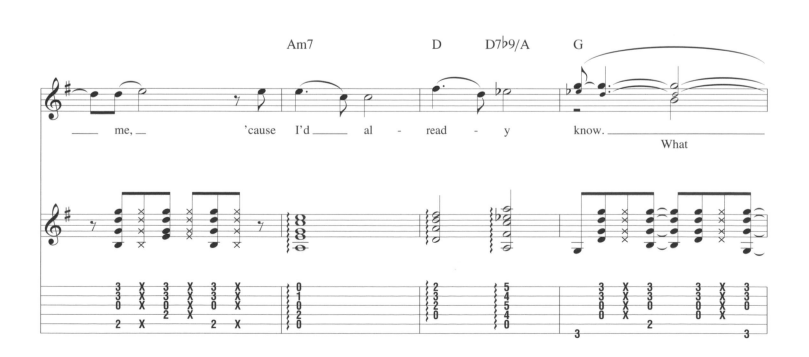

____ me, ___ 'cause I'd _____ al - read - y know. _____

What

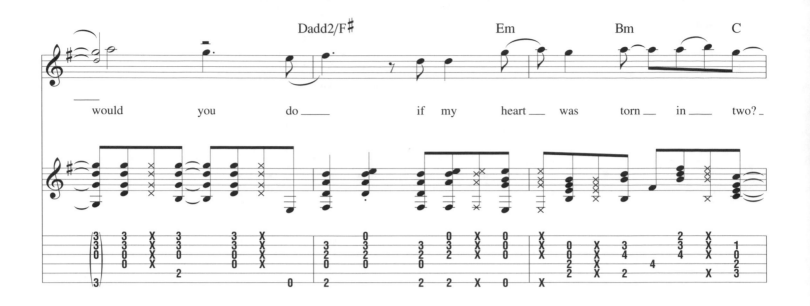

would you do ___ if my heart ___ was torn ___ in ___ two? ___

___ More than words ___ to show ___ you feel ___ that your love ___

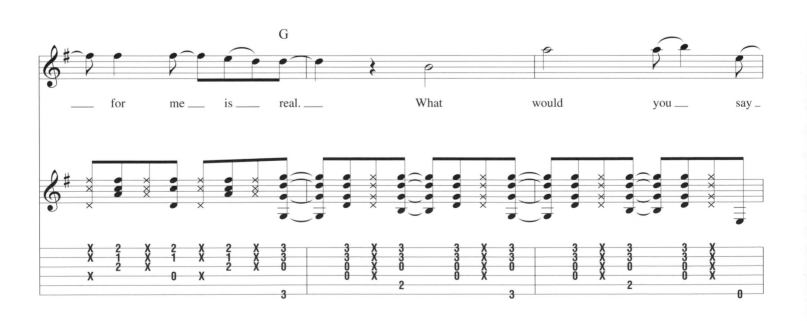

___ for me ___ is ___ real. ___ What would you ___ say ___

if I took those words a - way? Then you could-

-n't make things new just by say - ing "I love

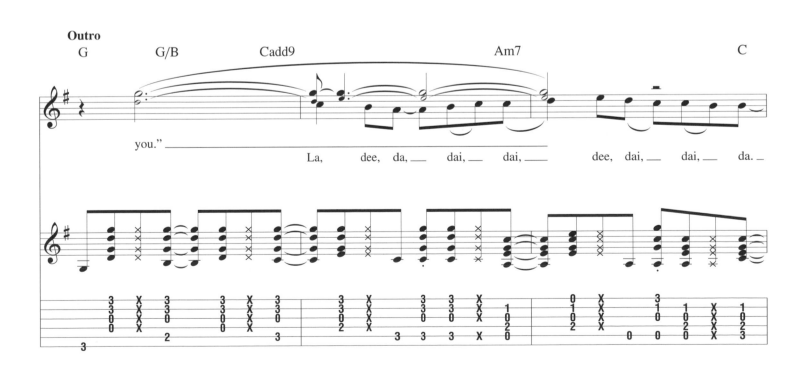

Outro

you." La, dee, da, dai, dai, dee, dai, dai, da.

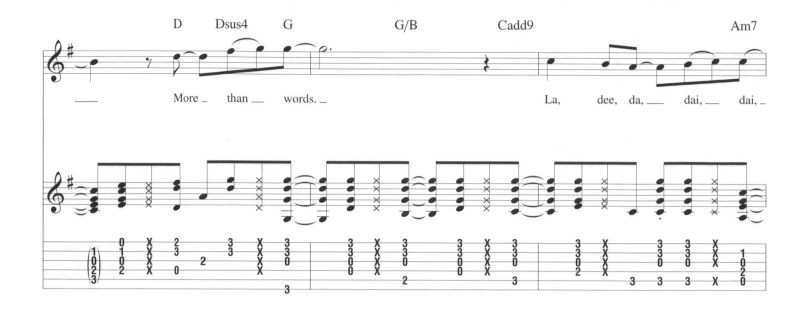

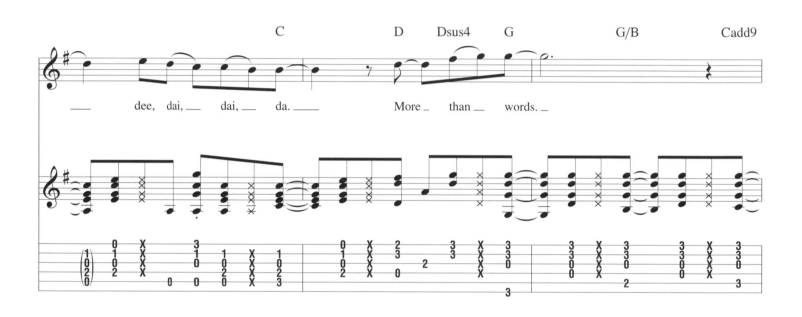

La, da, da, dai, da.
La, da, da, dai, da. La,

strum - - ⊣ Slap body

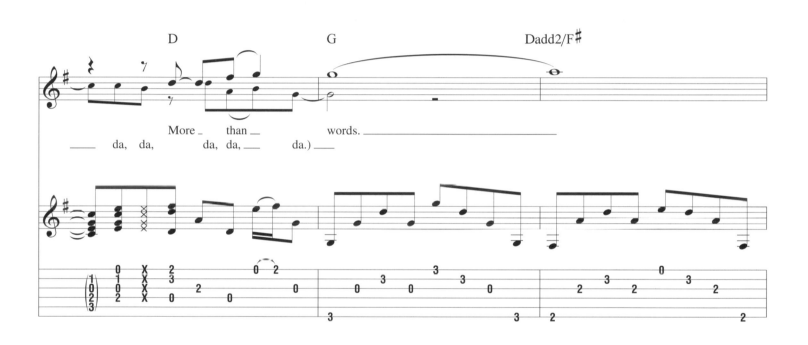

More than words.
da, da, da, da, da.)

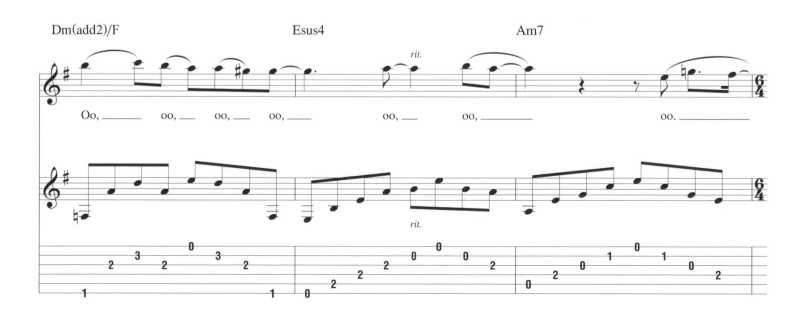

Oo, oo, oo, oo, oo, oo, oo.

PATIENCE
Guns N' Roses

Video Lesson – 23 minutes, 13 seconds

Tune Down 1/2 Step: (low to high) E♭–A♭–D♭–G♭–B♭–E♭
Key of G, D

Guitar Tone:

- steel-string acoustic guitar

Chords:

Intro/Verse/Chorus:

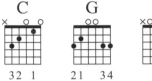

C   G   A   D   Em

32 1   21   34   1 2 3   1 3 2   1 2

Outro:

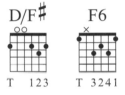

D/F♯   F6

T   1 2 3   T   3 2 4 1

Scales:

Guitar Solos:

G Major Scale

7fr

Techniques:

- Strumming: it's not necessary to strum all the notes of each chord every time. Strive for a loose strumming feel, striking only some of the strings within each chord. This will sound more natural and musical. Generally, downstrokes tend to catch the lower three strings and upstrokes catch the higher three strings.

- Thumb-Fretting: for the D/F♯ and F6 chords in the Outro, wrap your fret-hand thumb over the neck to fret the bass notes on the 6th string. If you're not comfortable using your thumb, you can use your 1st finger instead, but it makes the chords more difficult to fret.

- Dyads: for the 6th intervals in the opening Guitar Solo, fret the notes on the 3rd string with the middle finger and the notes on the 1st string with the ring or index (depending on the shape). Your middle finger should be lightly touching the 2nd string to mute it. Then you can strum through the top three strings for each dyad and only two strings will produce sound.

- String Bending: on an acoustic guitar, bends are usually more difficult because of the higher tension and thicker strings. Be sure to use support fingers behind the bending finger to add some strength. You can also try lighter gauge strings. Another alternative is to replace the bends with slides if you just can't get those strings bent up to pitch.

Patience

Words and Music by W. Axl Rose, Slash, Izzy Stradlin', Duff McKagan and Steven Adler

Tune down 1/2 step:
(low to high) E♭-A♭-D♭-G♭-B♭-E♭

Intro
Moderate Rock ♩ = 120
Half-time feel

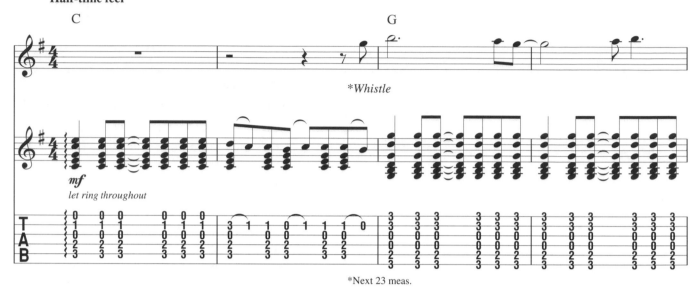

*Whistle

*Next 23 meas.

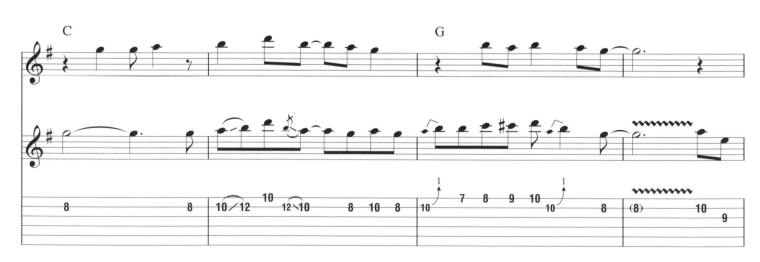

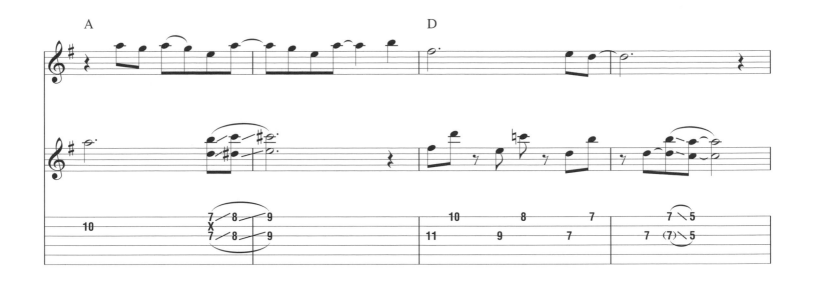

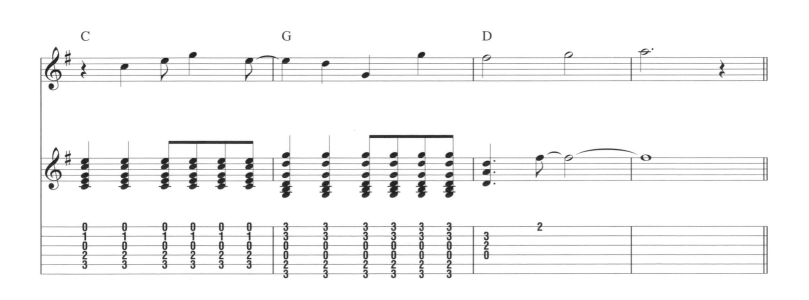

Verse

1. Shed a tear 'cause I'm miss - in' ___ you, ___ I'm still al - right ___ to smile. ___
2. *See additional lyrics*

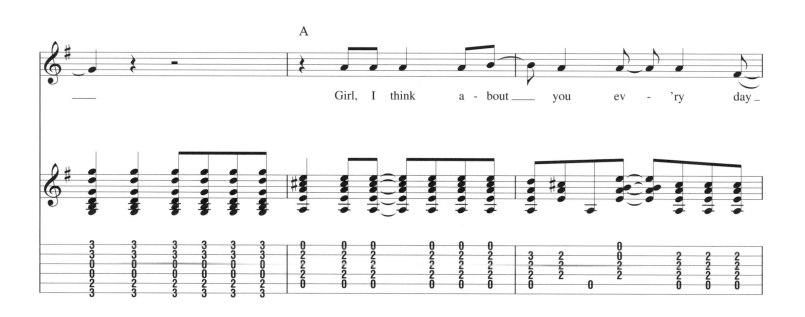

___ Girl, I think a - bout ___ you ev - 'ry day ___

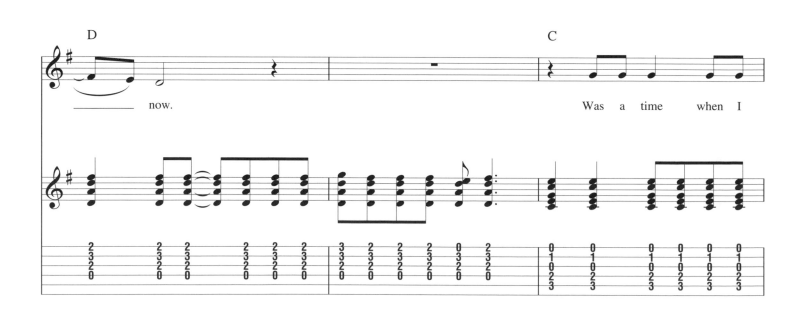

___ now. Was a time when I

was - n't ___ sure ___ but you ___ set my mind ___ at ease. ___

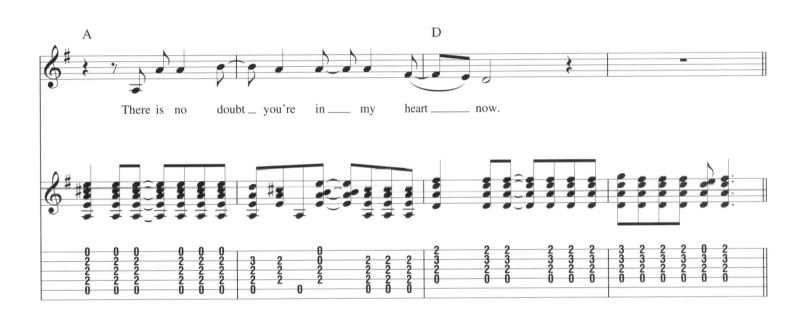

There is no doubt ___ you're in ___ my heart ___ now.

Chorus

Said, wom - an, ___ take it slow, ___ it - 'll work it - self ___ out fine. ___
See additional lyrics

All we need ___ is just a lit - tle pa -

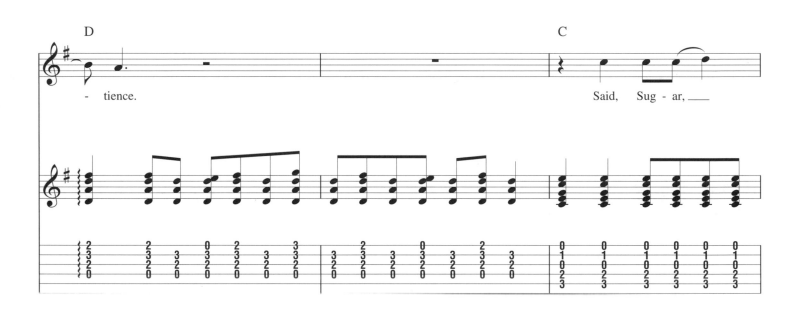

- tience. Said, Sug - ar, ___

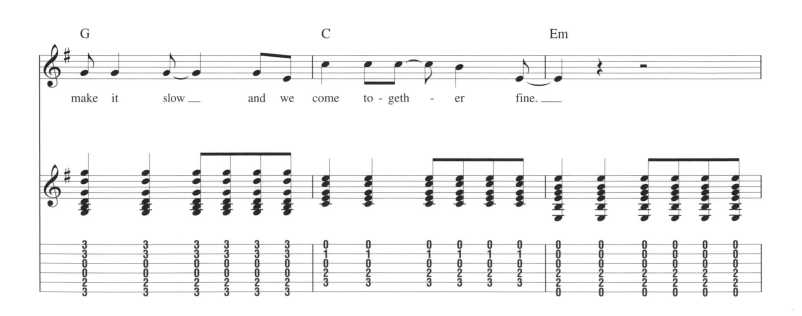

make it slow ___ and we come to - geth - er fine. ___

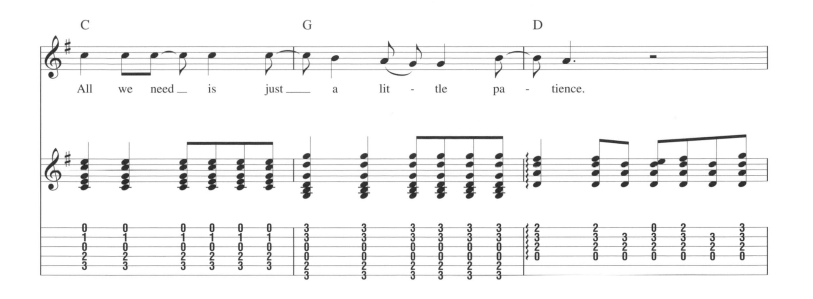

All we need __ is just ____ a lit - tle pa - tience.

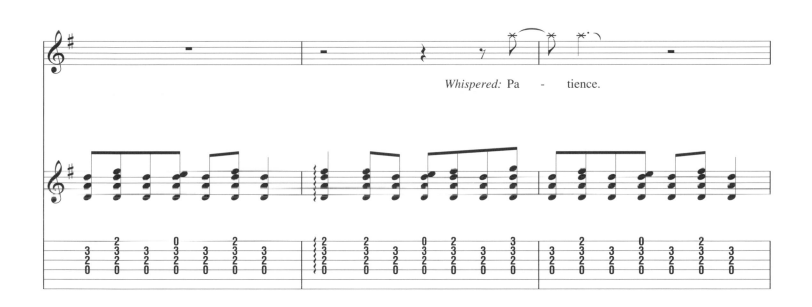

Whispered: Pa - tience.

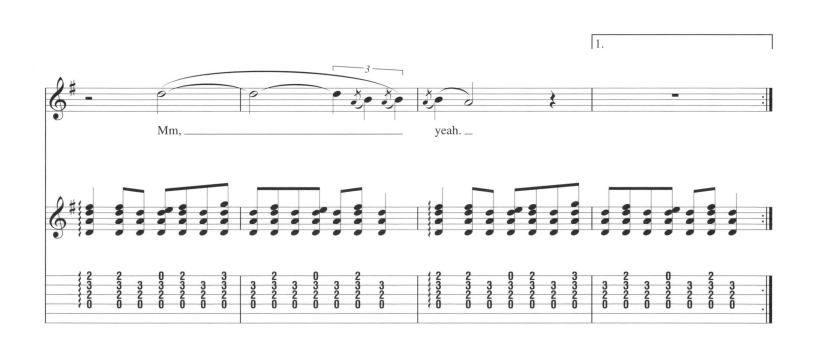

Mm, _____ yeah. __

Guitar Solo

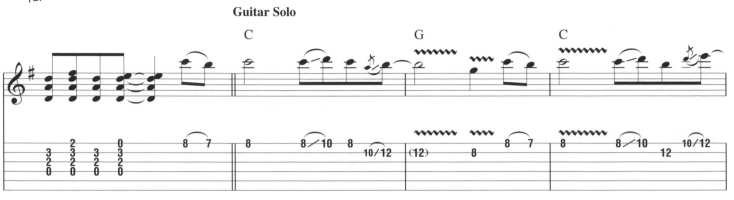

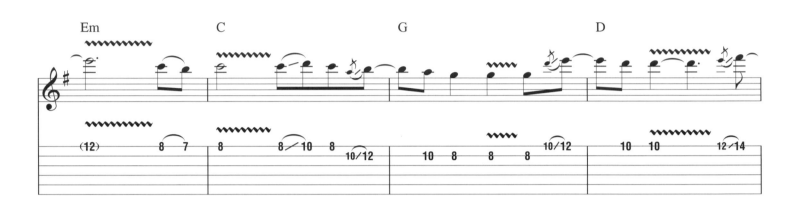

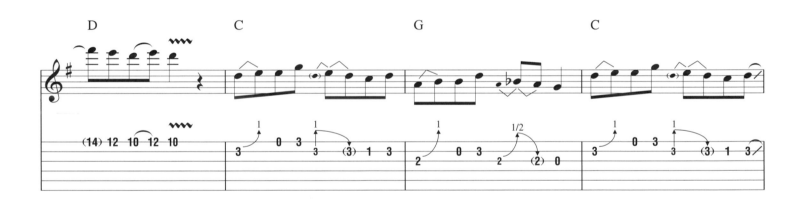

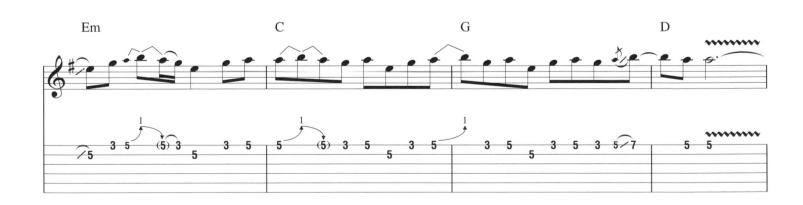

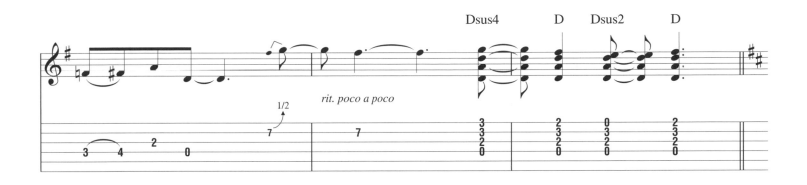

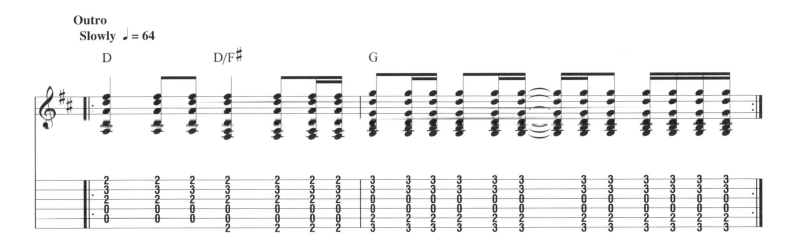

Outro
Slowly ♩ = 64

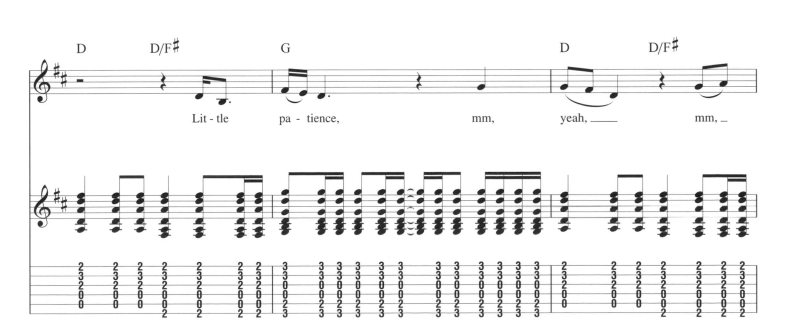

Lit - tle   pa - tience,   mm,   yeah, _____   mm, _

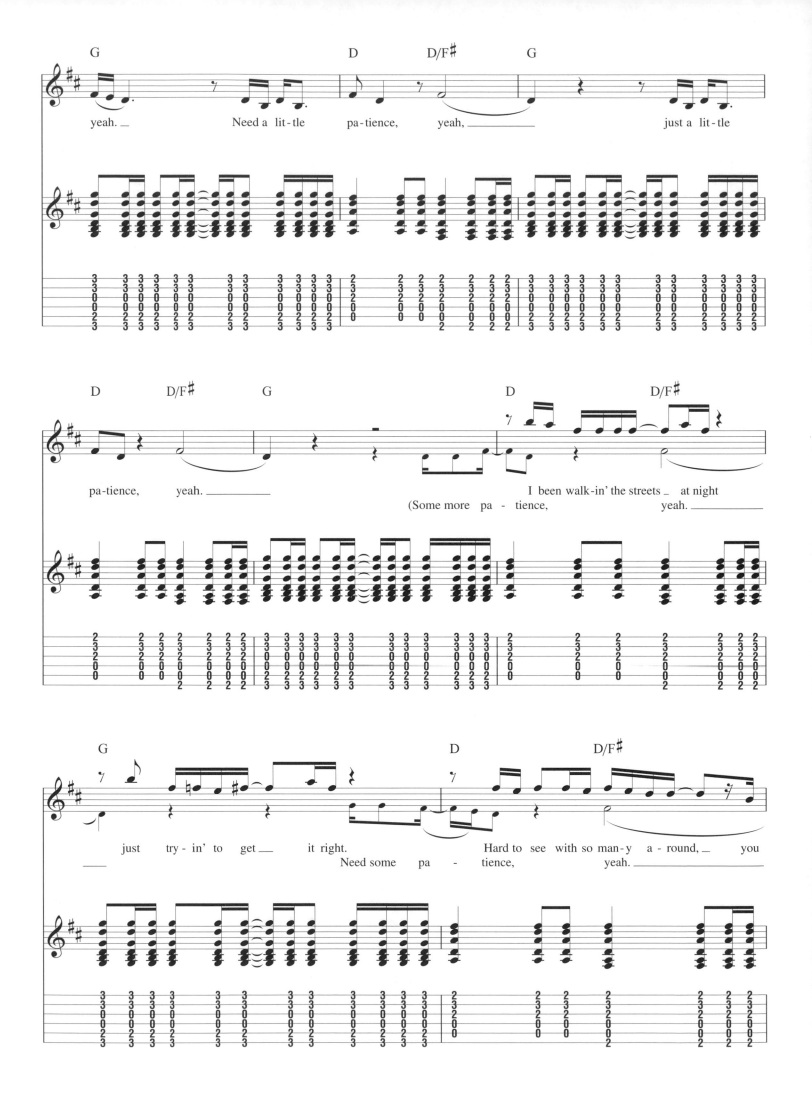

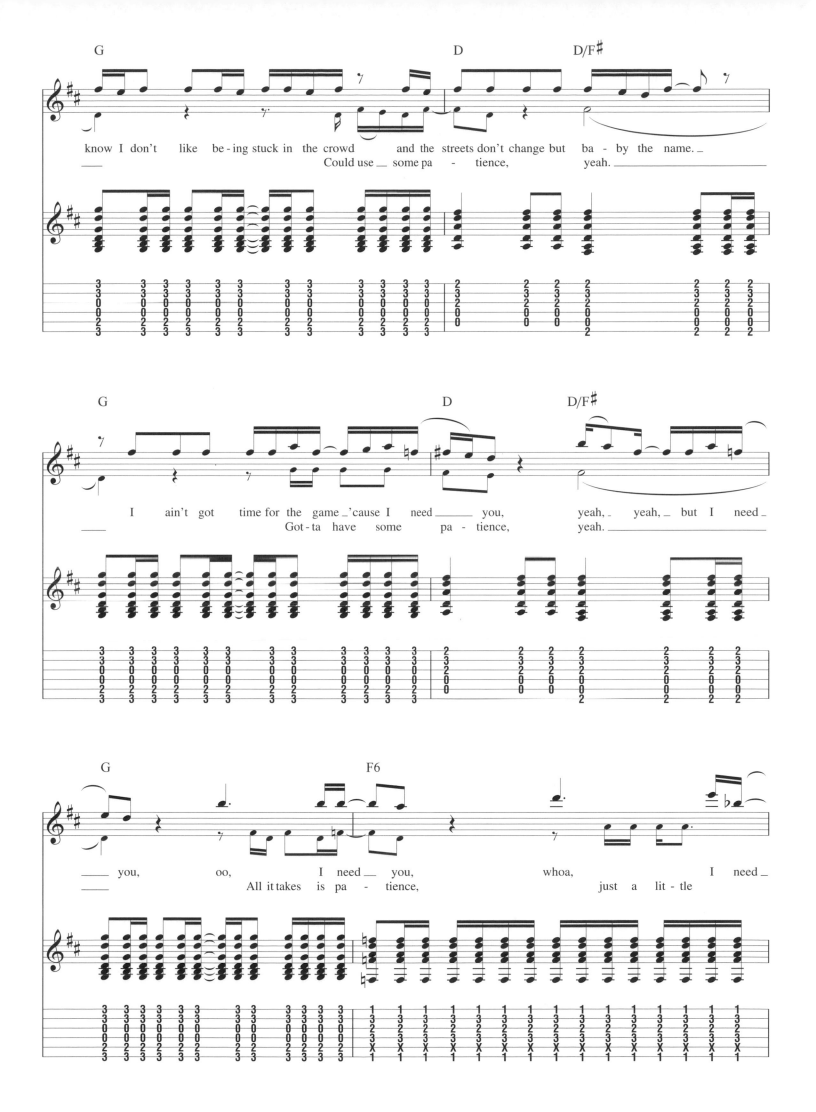

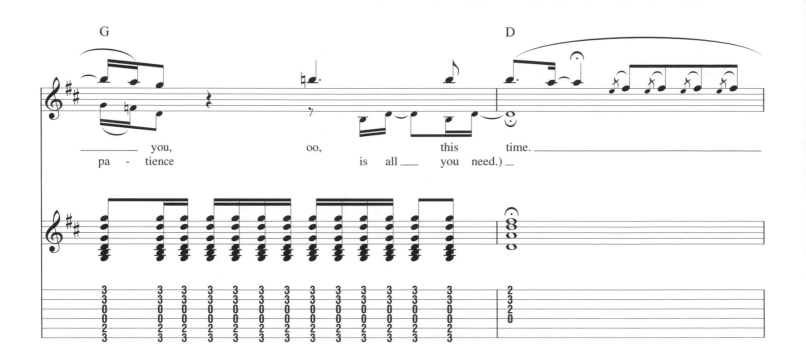

you,   oo,   this   time.

pa - tience   is   all   you   need.)

Free time

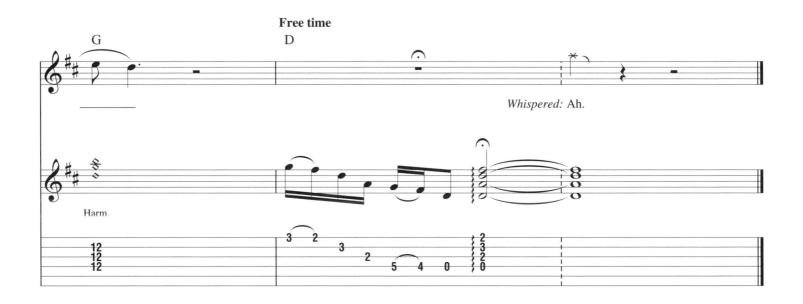

Whispered: Ah.

Harm.

Additional Lyrics

2. I sit here on the stairs 'cause I'd rather be alone.
   If I can't have you right now I'll wait, dear.
   Sometimes I get so tense but I can't speed up the time.
   But you know, love, there's one more thing to consider.

Chorus Said, woman, take it slow and things will be just fine.
   You and I'll just use a little patience.
   Said, Sugar, take the time 'cause the lights are shining bright.
   You and I've got what it takes to make it.
   We won't fake it, ah, I'll never break it 'cause I can't take it.

WONDERWALL
Oasis

Video Lesson – 13 minutes, 10 seconds

Standard Tuning: (low to high) E–A–D–G–B–E
Key of A (capo II)

Guitar Tone:

- steel-string acoustic guitar

- capo at 2nd fret

Chords/Arpeggios:

Intro/Verse/Chorus:

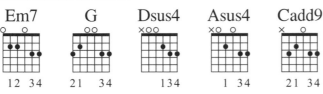

Pre-Chorus:

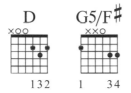

Techniques:

- Strumming: it's not necessary to strum all the notes of each chord every time. Strive for a loose strumming feel, striking only some of the strings within each chord. This will sound more natural and musical. Generally, downstrokes tend to catch the lower three strings and upstrokes catch the higher three strings.

- Common Tones: almost every chord in this song includes the notes D and G on the top two strings. Keep your ring and pinky fingers planted here throughout to make the chord changes nice and smooth while keeping these droning tones constant.

- Arpeggios: in the Pre-Chorus, hold down the full chord shapes for each chord change while you arpeggiate them. Keep your fingers arched so you don't inadvertently mute any strings.

Wonderwall

Words and Music by Noel Gallagher

Capo II

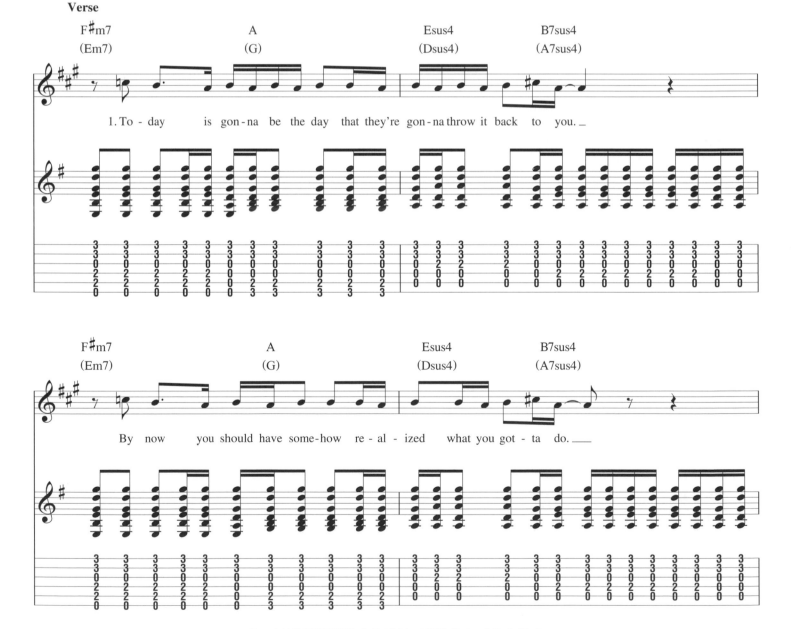

*Symbols in parentheses represent chord names respective to capoed guitar.
Symbols above reflect actual sounding chords. Capoed fret is "0" in tab.

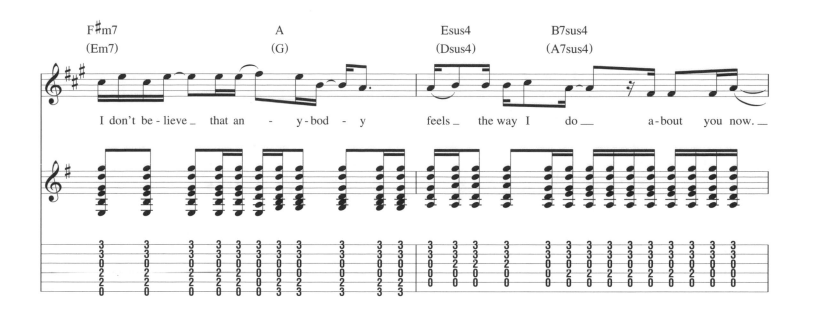

I don't be-lieve _ that an - - y-bod - y feels _ the way I do _ a-bout you now. _

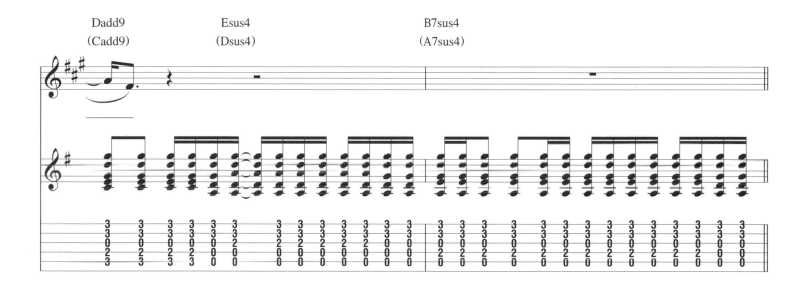

Verse

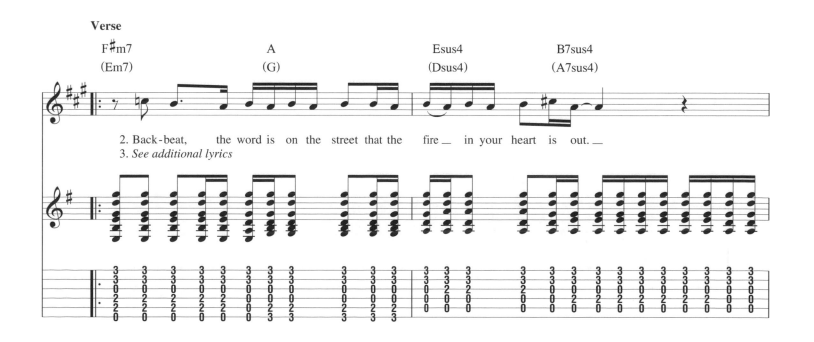

2. Back-beat, the word is on the street that the fire _ in your heart is out. _
3. *See additional lyrics*

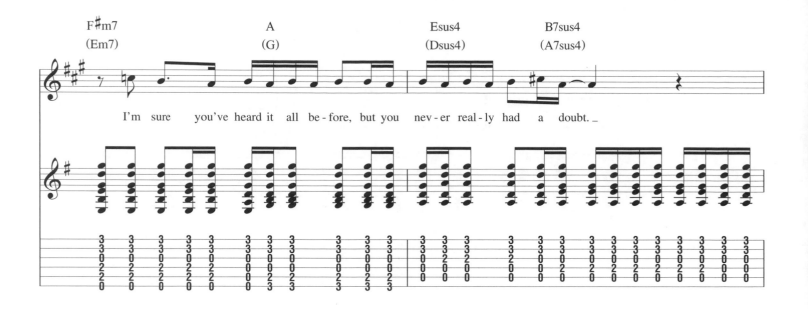

I'm sure   you've heard it   all be-fore, but you   nev-er real-ly had   a   doubt. _

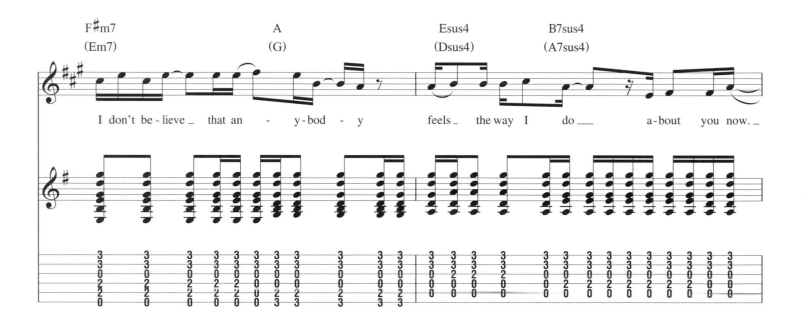

I   don't be-lieve _   that   an   -   y-bod   -   y   feels _   the way I   do _   a-bout   you now. _

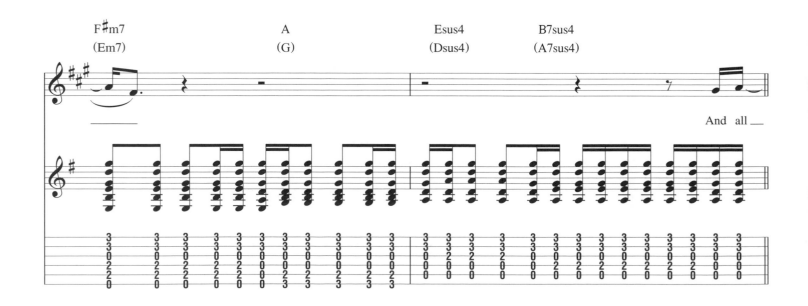

_____ And   all __

Pre-Chorus

_____ the roads _ we have _ to walk _ are wind - ing, and all __

See additional lyrics

let chords ring throughout

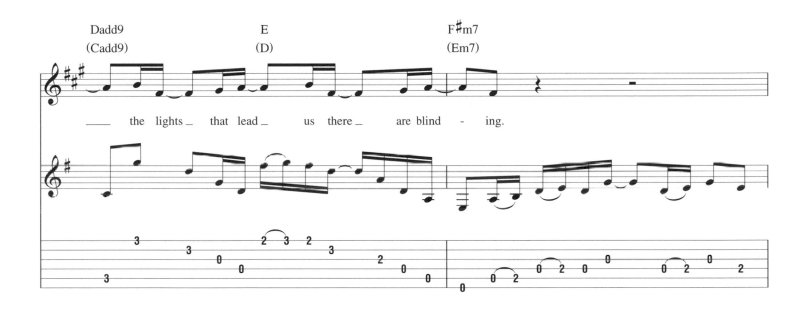

_____ the lights _ that lead _ us there _ are blind - ing.

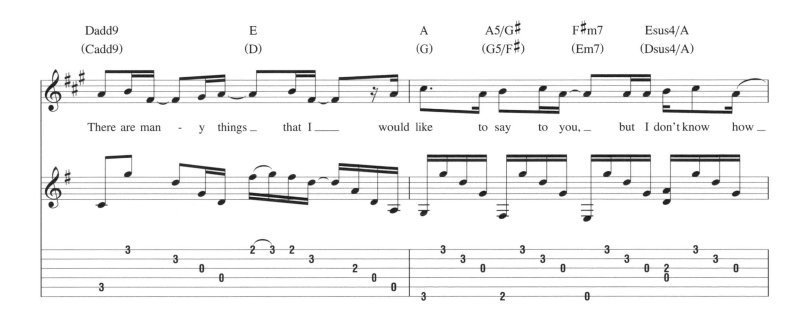

There are man - y things _ that I ____ would like to say to you, _ but I don't know how _

Chorus

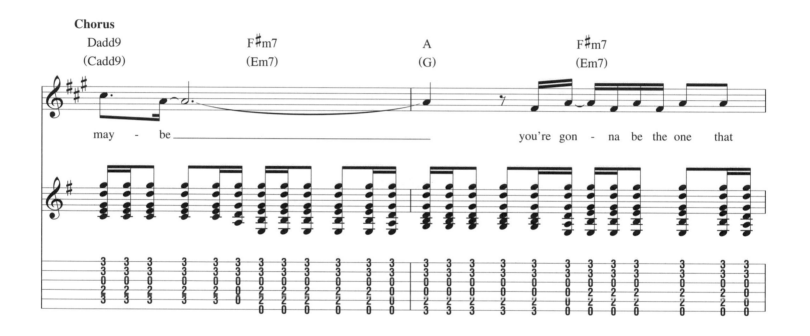

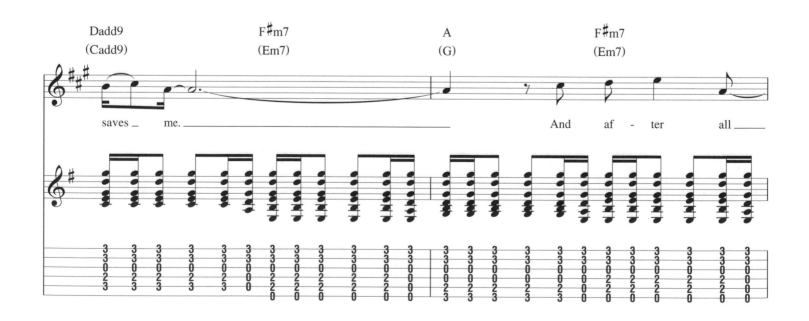

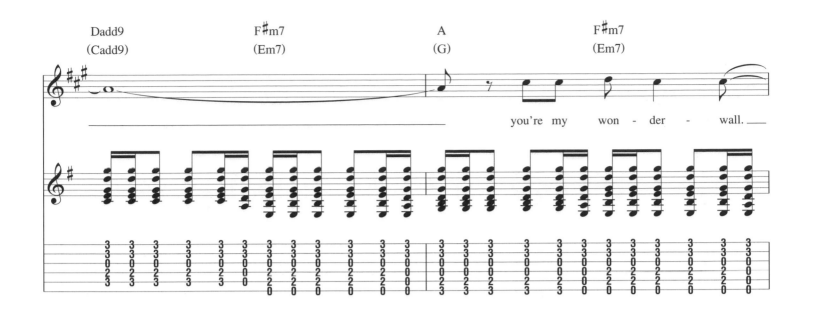

you're my won - der - wall. ___

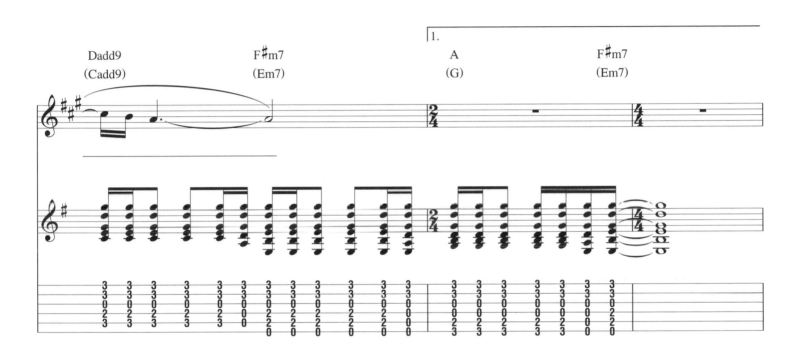

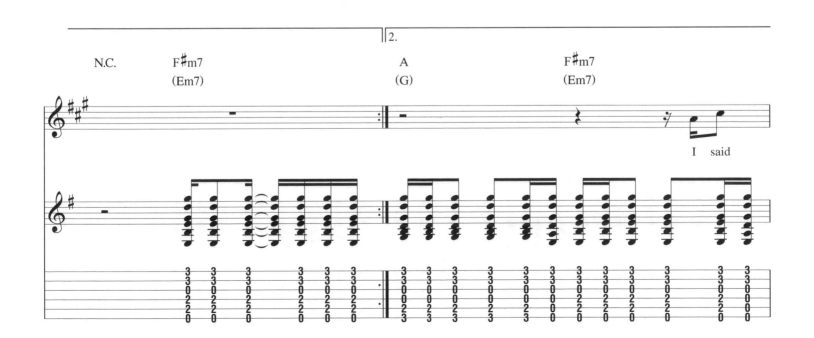

I said

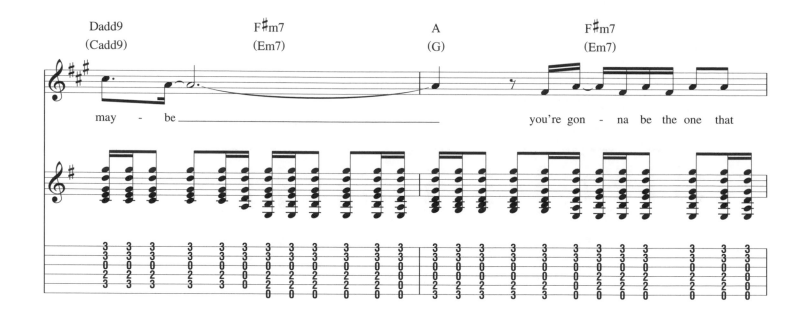

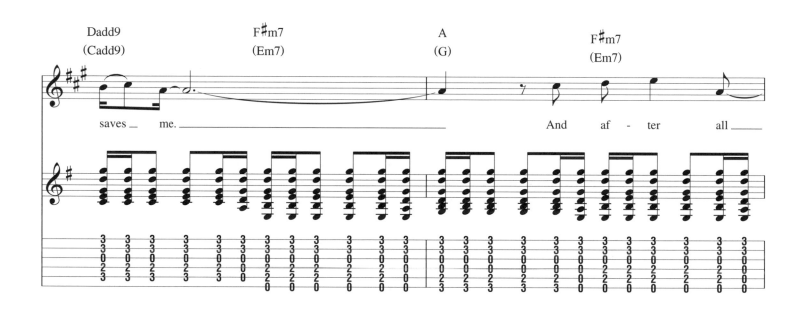

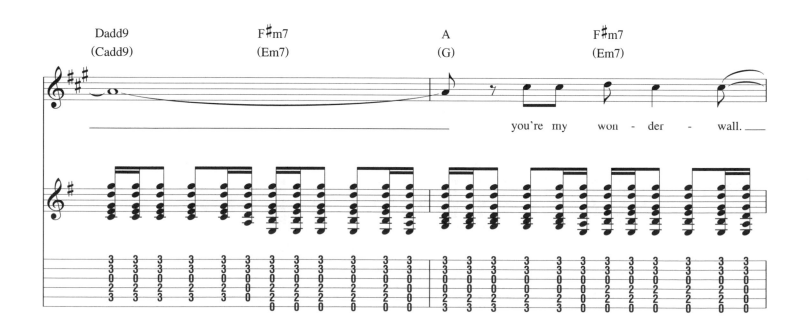

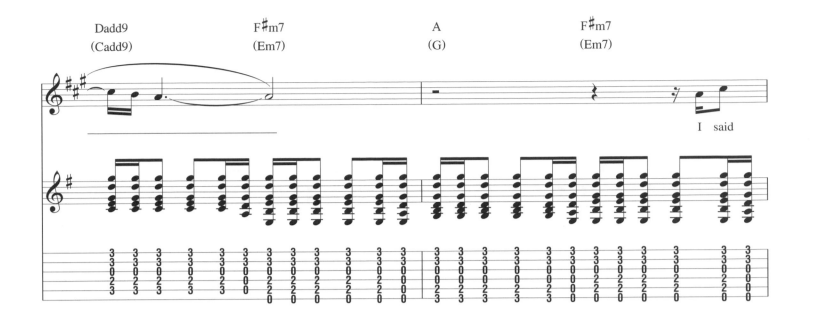

I said

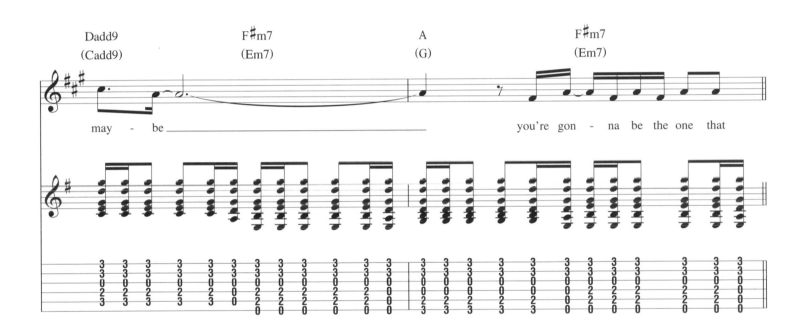

may - be _____ you're gon - na be the one that

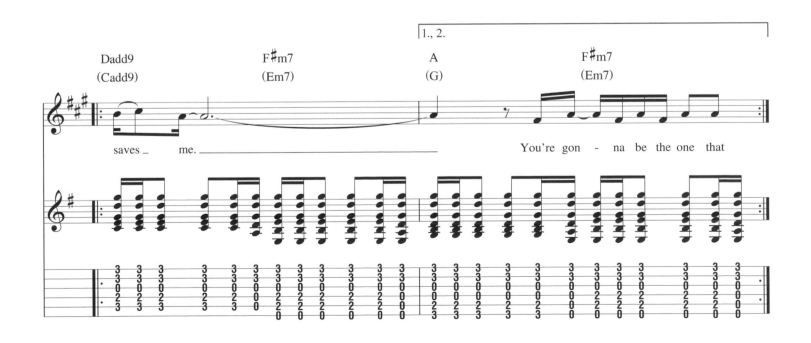

saves _ me. _____ You're gon - na be the one that

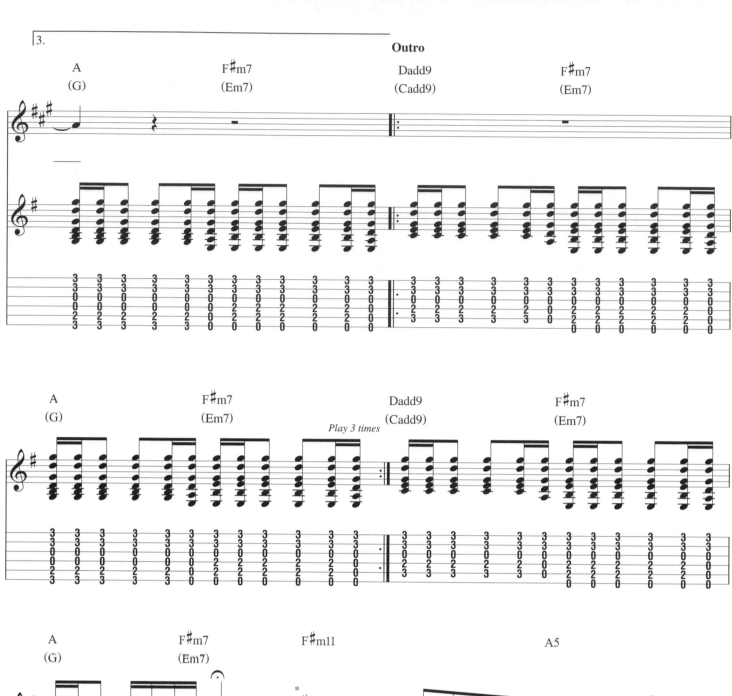

*Remove capo.

Additional Lyrics

3. Today was gonna be the day, but they'll never throw it back to you.
By now you should have somehow realized what you're not to do.
I don't believe that anybody feels the way I do about you now.

Pre-Chorus And all the roads that lead you there were winding,
And all the lights that light the way are blinding.
There are many things that I would like to say to you,
But I don't know how.
I said...

YOU WERE MEANT FOR ME
Jewel

Video Lesson – 11 minutes, 46 seconds

Tune Down 1/2 Step: (low to high) E♭–A♭–D♭–G♭–B♭–E♭
Key of G

Guitar Tone:

- steel-string acoustic guitar

Chords/Arpeggios:

Intro/Verse:

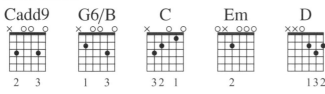

Chorus:

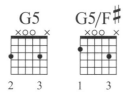

Bridge:

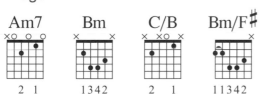

Techniques:

- Fingerpicking: in general, use your thumb to pluck the bass notes on the lower three strings, and your index, middle, and ring fingers to pluck the 3rd, 2nd, and 1st strings, respectively.

- Arpeggios: almost the entire song is arpeggiated, meaning chords are played one note at a time. Keep your fingers arched so you don't inadvertently mute any strings. Strive for a clean, clear attack on each note.

- Shuffle Feel: this song is played with a shuffle feel (or swing feel). This means all 8th notes are played in an uneven, long-short rhythm.

- Fingernails, Flesh, and Fingerpicks: there are several ways you can pluck the strings with your fingers. Fingernails sound great and can provide a consistent, clean attack, but you'll need to keep them well-buffed and filed so they are smooth and curved naturally around the fingertips. Some players will use just the flesh of their fingertips to pluck; this has its advantages as well. The sound is less consistent, but warmer and more organic, plus you don't have the nail maintenance. Another alternative are a thumbpick and fingerpicks, similar to a banjo player. These create a consistent sound and don't require upkeep, but do take some time to get used to.

You Were Meant for Me

Words and Music by Jewel Murray and Steve Poltz

Tune down 1/2 step:
(low to high) E♭-A♭-D♭-G♭-B♭-E♭

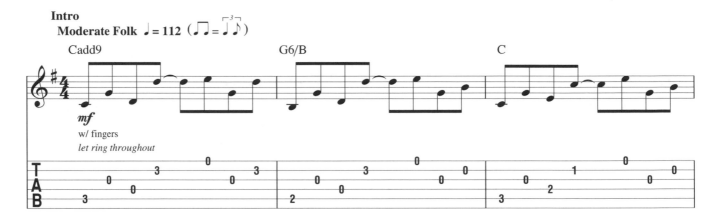

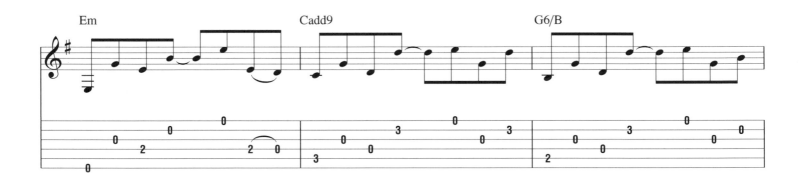

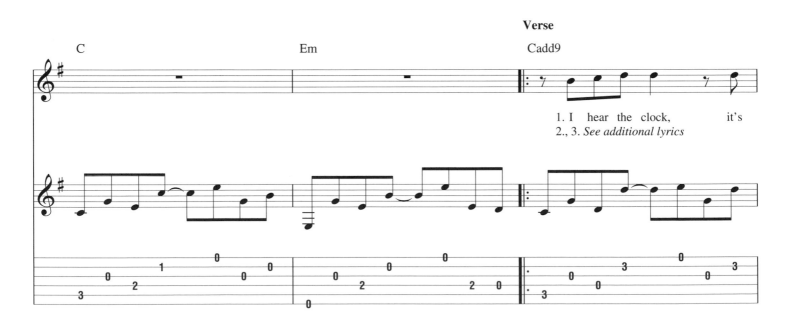

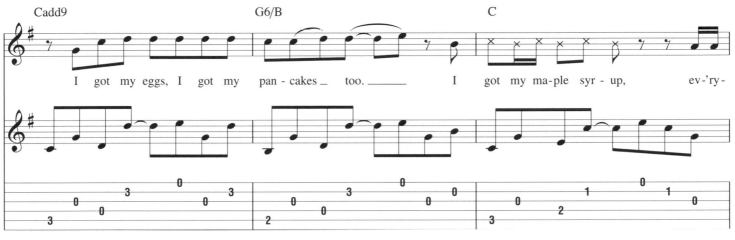

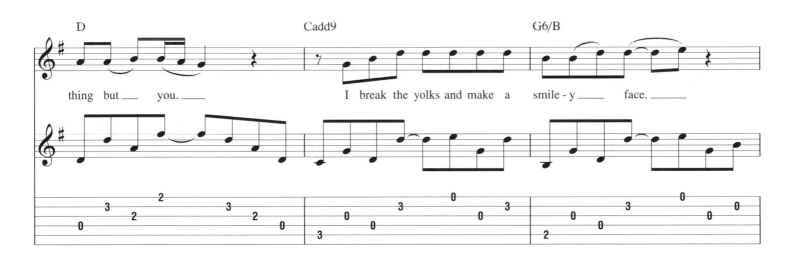

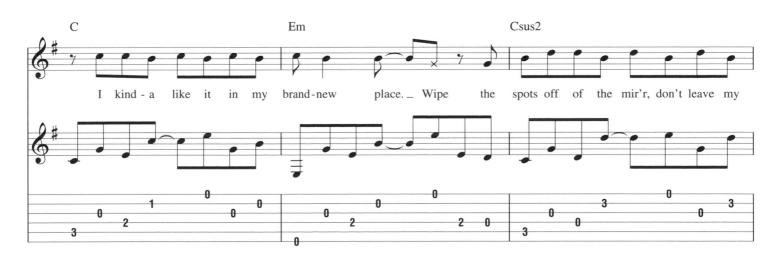

keys in the door.____ I nev-er put wet tow-els on the floor an-y-more_ 'cause

Chorus

dreams__ last__ so__ long,__ e - ven af - ter you're gone.__

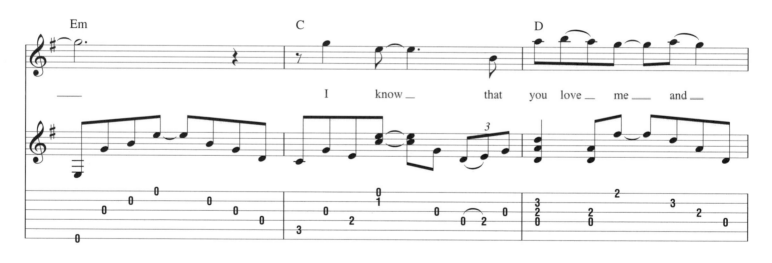

I know__ that you love__ me__ and__

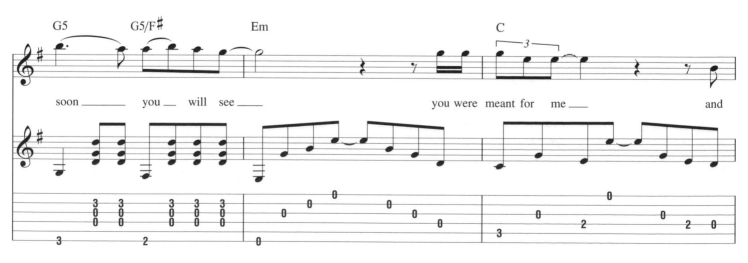

soon_____ you__ will see____ you were meant for me__ and

Outro

Additional Lyrics

2. I called my momma, she was out for a walk.
   Consoled a cup of coffee but it didn't wanna talk.
   So I picked up the paper, it was more bad news;
   More hearts being broken or people being used.
   Put on my coat in the pouring rain.
   I saw a movie, it just wasn't the same
   'Cause it was happy, oh, I was sad
   And it made me miss you, oh, so bad 'cause...

3. I brush my teeth, I put the cap back on.
   I know you hate it when I leave the light on.
   I pick a book up and then I turn the sheets down
   And then I take a deep breath and a good look around.
   Put on my PJs and hop into bed.
   I'm half alive but I feel mostly dead.
   I try and tell myself it'll all be alright.
   I just shouldn't think anymore tonight 'cause...

GUITAR NOTATION LEGEND

THE MUSICAL STAFF shows pitches and rhythms and is divided by bar lines into measures. Pitches are named after the first seven letters of the alphabet.

TABLATURE graphically represents the guitar fingerboard. Each horizontal line represents a string, and each number represents a fret.

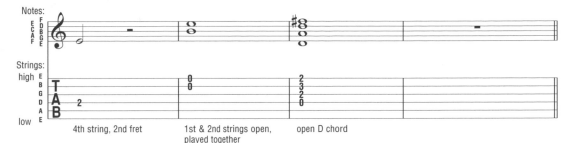

4th string, 2nd fret

1st & 2nd strings open, played together

open D chord

HALF-STEP BEND: Strike the note and bend up 1/2 step.

WHOLE-STEP BEND: Strike the note and bend up one step.

GRACE NOTE BEND: Strike the note and immediately bend up as indicated.

SLIGHT (MICROTONE) BEND: Strike the note and bend up 1/4 step.

BEND AND RELEASE: Strike the note and bend up as indicated, then release back to the original note. Only the first note is struck.

PRE-BEND: Bend the note as indicated, then strike it.

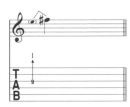

VIBRATO: The string is vibrated by rapidly bending and releasing the note with the fretting hand.

PALM MUTING: The note is partially muted by the pick hand lightly touching the string(s) just before the bridge.

HAMMER-ON: Strike the first (lower) note with one finger, then sound the higher note (on the same string) with another finger by fretting it without picking.

PULL-OFF: Place both fingers on the notes to be sounded. Strike the first note and without picking, pull the finger off to sound the second (lower) note.

LEGATO SLIDE: Strike the first note and then slide the same fret-hand finger up or down to the second note. The second note is not struck.

SHIFT SLIDE: Same as legato slide, except the second note is struck.

TRILL: Very rapidly alternate between the notes indicated by continuously hammering on and pulling off.

TAPPING: Hammer ("tap") the fret indicated with the pick-hand index or middle finger and pull off to the note fretted by the fret hand.

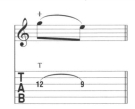

NATURAL HARMONIC: Strike the note while the fret-hand lightly touches the string directly over the fret indicated.

PINCH HARMONIC: The note is fretted normally and a harmonic is produced by adding the edge of the thumb or the tip of the index finger of the pick hand to the normal pick attack.

TREMOLO PICKING: The note is picked as rapidly and continuously as possible.

VIBRATO BAR DIVE AND RETURN: The pitch of the note or chord is dropped a specified number of steps (in rhythm), then returned to the original pitch.

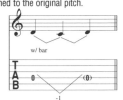

VIBRATO BAR SCOOP: Depress the bar just before striking the note, then quickly release the bar.

VIBRATO BAR DIP: Strike the note and then immediately drop a specified number of steps, then release back to the original pitch.

Additional Musical Definitions

(accent)   • Accentuate note (play it louder).

(staccato)   • Play the note short.

D.S. al Coda   • Go back to the sign (𝄋), then play until the measure marked "*To Coda*," then skip to the section labelled "**Coda.**"

D.C. al Fine   • Go back to the beginning of the song and play until the measure marked "***Fine***" (end).

Fill
• Label used to identify a brief melodic figure which is to be inserted into the arrangement.

N.C.
• Harmony is implied.

• Repeat measures between signs.

• When a repeated section has different endings, play the first ending only the first time and the second ending only the second time.

HAL•LEONARD GUITAR PLAY·ALONG

This series will help you play your favorite songs quickly and easily. Just follow the tab and listen to the audio to the hear how the guitar should sound, and then play along using the separate backing tracks. Mac or PC users can also slow down the tempo without changing pitch by using the CD in their computer. The melody and lyrics are included in the book so that you can sing or simply follow along.

INCLUDES TAB

VOL. 1 – ROCK	00699570 / $16.99
VOL. 2 – ACOUSTIC	00699569 / $16.95
VOL. 3 – HARD ROCK	00699573 / $16.95
VOL. 4 – POP/ROCK	00699571 / $16.99
VOL. 5 – MODERN ROCK	00699574 / $16.99
VOL. 6 – '90S ROCK	00699572 / $16.99
VOL. 7 – BLUES	00699575 / $16.95
VOL. 8 – ROCK	00699585 / $14.99
VOL. 10 – ACOUSTIC	00699586 / $16.95
VOL. 11 – EARLY ROCK	00699579 / $14.95
VOL. 12 – POP/ROCK	00699587 / $14.95
VOL. 13 – FOLK ROCK	00699581 / $15.99
VOL. 14 – BLUES ROCK	00699582 / $16.95
VOL. 15 – R&B	00699583 / $14.95
VOL. 16 – JAZZ	00699584 / $15.95
VOL. 17 – COUNTRY	00699588 / $15.95
VOL. 18 – ACOUSTIC ROCK	00699577 / $15.95
VOL. 19 – SOUL	00699578 / $14.99
VOL. 20 – ROCKABILLY	00699580 / $14.95
VOL. 21 – YULETIDE	00699602 / $14.95
VOL. 22 – CHRISTMAS	00699600 / $15.95
VOL. 23 – SURF	00699635 / $14.95
VOL. 24 – ERIC CLAPTON	00699649 / $17.99
VOL. 25 – LENNON & MCCARTNEY	00699642 / $16.99
VOL. 26 – ELVIS PRESLEY	00699643 / $14.95
VOL. 27 – DAVID LEE ROTH	00699645 / $16.95
VOL. 28 – GREG KOCH	00699646 / $14.95
VOL. 29 – BOB SEGER	00699647 / $15.99
VOL. 30 – KISS	00699644 / $16.99
VOL. 31 – CHRISTMAS HITS	00699652 / $14.95
VOL. 32 – THE OFFSPRING	00699653 / $14.95
VOL. 33 – ACOUSTIC CLASSICS	00699656 / $16.95
VOL. 34 – CLASSIC ROCK	00699658 / $16.95
VOL. 35 – HAIR METAL	00699660 / $16.95
VOL. 36 – SOUTHERN ROCK	00699661 / $16.95
VOL. 37 – ACOUSTIC UNPLUGGED	00699662 / $22.99
VOL. 38 – BLUES	00699663 / $16.95
VOL. 39 – '80S METAL	00699664 / $16.99
VOL. 40 – INCUBUS	00699668 / $17.95
VOL. 41 – ERIC CLAPTON	00699669 / $16.95
VOL. 42 – 2000S ROCK	00699670 / $16.99
VOL. 43 – LYNYRD SKYNYRD	00699681 / $17.95
VOL. 44 – JAZZ	00699689 / $14.99
VOL. 45 – TV THEMES	00699718 / $14.95
VOL. 46 – MAINSTREAM ROCK	00699722 / $16.95
VOL. 47 – HENDRIX SMASH HITS	00699723 / $19.95
VOL. 48 – AEROSMITH CLASSICS	00699724 / $17.99
VOL. 49 – STEVIE RAY VAUGHAN	00699725 / $17.99
VOL. 50 – VAN HALEN 1978-1984	00110269 / $17.99
VOL. 51 – ALTERNATIVE '90S	00699727 / $14.99
VOL. 52 – FUNK	00699728 / $14.95
VOL. 53 – DISCO	00699729 / $14.99
VOL. 54 – HEAVY METAL	00699730 / $14.95
VOL. 55 – POP METAL	00699731 / $14.95
VOL. 56 – FOO FIGHTERS	00699749 / $15.99
VOL. 57 – SYSTEM OF A DOWN	00699751 / $14.95
VOL. 58 – BLINK-182	00699772 / $14.95
VOL. 59 – CHET ATKINS	00702347 / $16.99
VOL. 60 – 3 DOORS DOWN	00699774 / $14.95
VOL. 61 – SLIPKNOT	00699775 / $16.99
VOL. 62 – CHRISTMAS CAROLS	00699798 / $12.95

VOL. 63 – CREEDENCE CLEARWATER REVIVAL	00699802 / $16.99
VOL. 64 – THE ULTIMATE OZZY OSBOURNE	00699803 / $16.99
VOL. 66 – THE ROLLING STONES	00699807 / $16.95
VOL. 67 – BLACK SABBATH	00699808 / $16.99
VOL. 68 – PINK FLOYD – DARK SIDE OF THE MOON	00699809 / $16.99
VOL. 69 – ACOUSTIC FAVORITES	00699810 / $14.95
VOL. 70 – OZZY OSBOURNE	00699805 / $16.99
VOL. 71 – CHRISTIAN ROCK	00699824 / $14.95
VOL. 73 – BLUESY ROCK	00699829 / $16.99
VOL. 75 – TOM PETTY	00699882 / $16.99
VOL. 76 – COUNTRY HITS	00699884 / $14.95
VOL. 77 – BLUEGRASS	00699910 / $12.99
VOL. 78 – NIRVANA	00700132 / $16.99
VOL. 79 – NEIL YOUNG	00700133 / $24.99
VOL. 80 – ACOUSTIC ANTHOLOGY	00700175 / $19.95
VOL. 81 – ROCK ANTHOLOGY	00700176 / $22.99
VOL. 82 – EASY SONGS	00700177 / $12.99
VOL. 83 – THREE CHORD SONGS	00700178 / $16.99
VOL. 84 – STEELY DAN	00700200 / $16.99
VOL. 85 – THE POLICE	00700269 / $16.99
VOL. 86 – BOSTON	00700465 / $16.99
VOL. 87 – ACOUSTIC WOMEN	00700763 / $14.99
VOL. 88 – GRUNGE	00700467 / $16.99
VOL. 89 – REGGAE	00700468 / $15.99
VOL. 90 – CLASSICAL POP	00700469 / $14.99
VOL. 91 – BLUES INSTRUMENTALS	00700505 / $14.99
VOL. 92 – EARLY ROCK INSTRUMENTALS	00700506 / $14.99
VOL. 93 – ROCK INSTRUMENTALS	00700507 / $16.99
VOL. 94 – SLOW BLUES	00700508 / $16.99
VOL. 95 – BLUES CLASSICS	00700509 / $14.99
VOL. 96 – THIRD DAY	00700560 / $14.95
VOL. 97 – ROCK BAND	00700703 / $14.99
VOL. 99 – ZZ TOP	00700762 / $16.99
VOL. 100 – B.B. KING	00700466 / $16.99
VOL. 101 – SONGS FOR BEGINNERS	00701917 / $14.99
VOL. 102 – CLASSIC PUNK	00700769 / $14.99
VOL. 103 – SWITCHFOOT	00700773 / $16.99
VOL. 104 – DUANE ALLMAN	00700846 / $16.99
VOL. 105 – LATIN	00700939 / $16.99
VOL. 106 – WEEZER	00700958 / $14.99
VOL. 107 – CREAM	00701069 / $16.99
VOL. 108 – THE WHO	00701053 / $16.99
VOL. 109 – STEVE MILLER	00701054 / $14.99
VOL. 110 – SLIDE GUITAR HITS	00701055 / $16.99
VOL. 111 – JOHN MELLENCAMP	00701056 / $14.99
VOL. 112 – QUEEN	00701052 / $16.99
VOL. 113 – JIM CROCE	00701058 / $15.99
VOL. 114 – BON JOVI	00701060 / $14.99
VOL. 115 – JOHNNY CASH	00701070 / $16.99
VOL. 116 – THE VENTURES	00701124 / $14.99
VOL. 117 – BRAD PAISLEY	00701224 / $16.99
VOL. 118 – ERIC JOHNSON	00701353 / $16.99
VOL. 119 – AC/DC CLASSICS	00701356 / $17.99
VOL. 120 – PROGRESSIVE ROCK	00701457 / $14.99
VOL. 121 – U2	00701508 / $16.99
VOL. 122 – CROSBY, STILLS & NASH	00701610 / $16.99
VOL. 123 – LENNON & MCCARTNEY ACOUSTIC	00701614 / $16.99
VOL. 125 – JEFF BECK	00701687 / $16.99

VOL. 126 – BOB MARLEY	00701701 / $16.99
VOL. 127 – 1970S ROCK	00701739 / $14.99
VOL. 128 – 1960S ROCK	00701740 / $14.99
VOL. 129 – MEGADETH	00701741 / $16.99
VOL. 131 – 1990S ROCK	00701743 / $14.99
VOL. 132 – COUNTRY ROCK	00701757 / $15.99
VOL. 133 – TAYLOR SWIFT	00701894 / $16.99
VOL. 134 – AVENGED SEVENFOLD	00701906 / $16.99
VOL. 136 – GUITAR THEMES	00701922 / $14.99
VOL. 137 – IRISH TUNES	00701966 / $15.99
VOL. 138 – BLUEGRASS CLASSICS	00701967 / $14.99
VOL. 139 – GARY MOORE	00702370 / $16.99
VOL. 140 – MORE STEVIE RAY VAUGHAN	00702396 / $17.99
VOL. 141 – ACOUSTIC HITS	00702401 / $16.99
VOL. 143 – SLASH	00702425 / $19.99
VOL. 144 – DJANGO REINHARDT	00702531 / $16.99
VOL. 145 – DEF LEPPARD	00702532 / $16.99
VOL. 146 – ROBERT JOHNSON	00702533 / $16.99
VOL. 147 – SIMON & GARFUNKEL	14041591 / $16.99
VOL. 148 – BOB DYLAN	14041592 / $16.99
VOL. 149 – AC/DC HITS	14041593 / $17.99
VOL. 150 – ZAKK WYLDE	02501717 / $16.99
VOL. 152 – JOE BONAMASSA	02501751 / $19.99
VOL. 153 – RED HOT CHILI PEPPERS	00702990 / $19.99
VOL. 155 – ERIC CLAPTON – FROM THE ALBUM UNPLUGGED	00703085 / $16.99
VOL. 156 – SLAYER	00703770 / $17.99
VOL. 157 – FLEETWOOD MAC	00101382 / $16.99
VOL. 158 – ULTIMATE CHRISTMAS	00101889 / $14.99
VOL. 159 – WES MONTGOMERY	00102593 / $19.99
VOL. 160 – T-BONE WALKER	00102641 / $16.99
VOL. 161 – THE EAGLES – ACOUSTIC	00102659 / $17.99
VOL. 162 – THE EAGLES HITS	00102667 / $17.99
VOL. 163 – PANTERA	00103036 / $17.99
VOL. 164 – VAN HALEN 1986-1995	00110270 / $17.99
VOL. 166 – MODERN BLUES	00700764 / $16.99
VOL. 168 – KISS	00113421 / $16.99
VOL. 169 – TAYLOR SWIFT	00115982 / $16.99
VOL. 170 – THREE DAYS GRACE	00117337 / $16.99
VOL. 171 – JAMES BROWN	00117420 / $16.99
VOL. 172 – THE DOOBIE BROTHERS	00119670 / $16.99
VOL. 174 – SCORPIONS	00122119 / $16.99
VOL. 175 – MICHAEL SCHENKER	00122127 / $16.99
VOL. 176 – BLUES BREAKERS WITH JOHN MAYALL & ERIC CLAPTON	00122132 / $19.99
VOL. 177 – ALBERT KING	00123271 / $16.99
VOL. 178 – JASON MRAZ	00124165 / $17.99
VOL. 179 – RAMONES	00127073 / $16.99
VOL. 180 – BRUNO MARS	00129706 / $16.99
VOL. 181 – JACK JOHNSON	00129854 / $16.99
VOL. 182 – SOUNDGARDEN	00138161 / $17.99
VOL. 184 – KENNY WAYNE SHEPHERD	00138258 / $17.99
VOL. 187 – JOHN DENVER	00140839 / $17.99

Complete song lists available online.

Prices, contents, and availability subject to change without notice.

HAL•LEONARD® CORPORATION

7777 W. BLUEMOUND RD. P.O. BOX 13819 MILWAUKEE, WI 53213

www.halleonard.com

1215